NAVI
WITH HUMOR

NAVIGATING GRIEF WITH HUMOR

Melissa Mork

This book is intended as information, not therapy. If you are in distress, please seek assistance through a grief support group, psychologist, or other mental health professional.

Printed in the United States of America
ISBN: 9781072194248

Cover photo provided by Bobeedy Photography
Author photo credit: Lynae Berge Wingate

Published by Kindle Direct Publishing
Navigating Grief with Humor, Melissa Mork - First edition.
Includes bibliographical information

Nonfiction > Self-Help > Death, Grief, Bereavement
Nonfiction > Humor > Topic > Relationships

To Scott

"I'm gonna love you forever and ever,
Forever and ever, amen."
~ Randy Travis

Am I Normal?

My grieving clients will ask me, "Is this normal?"

I'm never dismissive of the question. Like any good therapist, I answer their question with another question: "What is worrying you?"

But really, in the back of my head, I'm thinking, "What's 'normal' anyway?"

A young daughter was killed while riding her bicycle. In her grief, her mother can't remember how to turn on the shower. "Am I normal?"

A man's wife of sixty years died after a long battle with dementia. He feels closest to her when he carries her ashes with him in satchels around his neck, in his pockets, under his pillow. He whispers, "This can't be normal."

A widow was laughing with her friends at her husband's funeral. Was that normal?

After my mom was killed in a car crash my dad developed chills that were so severe his body shook as if he were having seizures. He looked at me as he tried to lift his coffee cup, sloshing hot coffee all over the table, and pleaded, "Is this normal?"

Shortly after that, my dad died of a broken heart. I'd been so concerned for him that I hadn't really grieved for my mom. So when he died, I grieved the cumulative loss of both of them together. Was that normal?

And when my strong, handsome husband died after a short battle with an aggressive cancer, leaving me to raise our two teens alone, I stood in my kitchen and howled like a wounded animal. I'd like to believe I am normal.

Who's to say what is normal? It's such a benign, ambiguous word. Such a dumb word: normal.

Normal comes from our idea of cultural or social norms, and our Western culture has presumed to prescribe what's normal, even in grief. Sadly, I think we are way wrong. Nobody wants to think about death. Talk about death.

We fear death so we erect defenses against it and pretend it will never happen to us. Everything about death is hidden or restrained.

As a result, we deny the reality of how hard this will be; we fail to set up protective traditions or norms, and as a result, our cultural norm is harmful to the grief process.

At our jobs, we get six to twelve weeks of maternity leave when we have a baby, but three days of bereavement leave when our child dies. Hopefully, one's employer will have a little empathy, but the reality of corporate America is that our loss is not their problem.

We have days to say goodbye to our child when we had weeks of maternity leave to say hello to him. Weeks to adjust to having her in our life, and days to adjust to not having her in our life.

We don't provide cultural traditions to communicate our loss to others. We no longer dress in black for a set amount of time to indicate our mourning.

Most of us don't wear emblems on our arms to signify to the grocery store clerk or other customers that we are broken hearted. We don't have a word to begin each conversation to alert others on the phone that we've endured the single-most significant loss of our lives.

Our friends and family might think they know what's normal. They might be wrong. When they tell you it's time to get over it, they *are* actually wrong.

When they, out of exasperation, demand, "How long do you plan on grieving?" they may be confused about the process.

When you bring up the name of your loved one and they meet you with awkward silence, my beloved friend, they are wronging you. They don't mean to, but it still hurts.

Truly, grief is awful. It's long and it's hard. In a household panel survey in Britain that has collected data since 1991, respondents agreed that bereavement is the most traumatic life event we endure (Clark & Georgellis, 2013).

The Holmes-Rahe Stress Inventory assesses one's stressors over a single year, adding up points to determine social readjustment and predicting stress-related health issues (Holmes & Rahe, 1967).

On a scale of 0-100, with 100 being the highest cause for stress one will endure, the death of a loved one scores the full 100. The next highest stressor is divorce at 73 points.

No doubt about it. Grief is hard. It's long. It's horrendous and awful.

But is it normal?

The patterns and processes of grief are as unique as the person who died, the cause of death, the length of illness or suddenness of loss, the type of relationship you had with that person, and your own personality.

What's normal about any of this? Everything about that relationship was unique to you, so your grief will be unique, as well.

Despite the many factors that make each person's grief unique, however, there are some common themes that emerge – yearning, crying, loneliness, aching in the chest, longing for the person who's gone.

At the beginning of our grief, most of us are able to function at maybe a 2.5 out of 10 (with 1 being paralyzed by distressing emotions and 10 is the joy of winning a big lottery).

Slowly we transition to a place where we can talk about the deceased without bursting into tears and making every other person uncomfortable in our presence (although, I have a pretty sick sense of humor and sometimes enjoy making people uncomfortable).

One of the ways we can begin to talk about our loss is to remember our loved one with good humor. We can recall the ways they made us laugh. We can talk about the ways we played together. Humor holds profound power in helping lift us when we are grieving.

As you and I move through this book, you will notice that I'm not actually very funny. That's because I'm an educator, not an entertainer, and generally speaking, college professors are rarely funny.

Regardless of the fact I'm not a stand-up comic, I enjoy humor. I look for it. I search it out. Whenever a chance arises, I will choose to laugh.

Please keep in mind there is so much more to good humor than being funny. Good humor includes positivity, gratitude, optimism, bravery, zest, hope, levity, and joy.

Throughout this book, I try to discuss grief with hope and levity and courage. I hope the content I bring you in the following chapters is saturated with optimism. I hope to help you find your resilience.

Much of what I will write in this book is related to my personal journey of grief. My parents died when I was still in college. My husband died when our children were still teens.

I certainly do not want to come across as self-indulgently navel-gazing. On the other hand, what I know about grief is directly tied to my personal experience with it. All that I know about grief is in the context through which I've lived it.

In my grief trajectory, humor, gratitude, and faith were the three most profound practices that built my resilience and allowed me to cope with my losses.

I pray you come away with the tools you need to locate your own resilience in the experiences of loss. I hope you will find purpose in your suffering and that you will do so with levity and joy.

Types of Grief

Wow, am I back-peddling! You're going to read this and say, "Hold the phone. You just said that we don't know what normal grief is, and now you're going to start listing *types* of grief? Work it out before you start writing about it, lady."

Yes, I know it's confusing, but despite an inability to define what normalcy *is*, theorists LOVE to come up with ways to identify what normalcy is *not*.

I'm not making this up when I tell you that grief theorists have identified at least ten (10) or more different kinds of grief. I'm only listing the most common types and will summarize them for you here.

Keep in mind, when I work with clients in grief counseling, the *last* thing I would ever do is systematically teach them the various types of grief. I listen to their story. I walk alongside them in their process, and if there is a type of grief listed here that might apply, I may discuss it with them.

Since I can't do that in person with you, I will cover these types here. If you find yourself reflected in one of these, you might want to drive over to your mental health professional (whoever is covered in your insurance network) and ask them if this sounds right. Then see if they can help you process through what you are experiencing.

Absent Grief

Mike's mother was in her sixties when she died unexpectedly of a brain aneurism. They had a fairly healthy relationship. He'd moved away to go to college and lived about three hours from his childhood home as an adult.

Mike got married, had kids, and would come home to visit once every few months. He and his wife spent Thanksgiving and Easter with his mom; Christmas and the 4th of July with the in-laws.

Mike didn't argue or fight with his mom. There was no conflict. He enjoyed her company, and she was proud of him. They would chat occasionally on the phone when something came up: an uncle was diagnosed with cancer, an old school friend got a promotion, that kind of thing.

When Mike's mother died, he was sad, of course. He cried at the funeral. He was sad that he had to sort through all of her things and sell her condo without her help or company.

Since her death, which was two years ago, he hasn't really had much of a grief response. He doesn't cry or ache for her. He misses her, but his sadness was never so heavy it felt like "grief."

Absent Grief seems to be a fairly common type of grief where the person doesn't show much disruption to his or her functioning. It might be the result of stuffing their feelings out of fear of feeling them, but more often this is the result of resilience.

The person wasn't depressed before or after the loss; he or she isn't avoidant or cold or aloof. Despite missing the person who is gone, the bereaved person continues to function well.

Abbreviated Grief

On the six-month anniversary of my husband's death, I went in for my routine medication infusion (I have an autoimmune disorder that requires I go to a hospital every six weeks for a medication drip that helps manage my symptoms).

My nurse asked me how I was doing, and I told her it was hard, that this was the six-month mark.

She commiserated with me briefly, and then she brightened, "So, are you dating now?"

Me: "Ummmm.... What?"

Nurse: "Yeah, you should start dating. It will take your mind off Scott."

Me: "Nnnnooooo. Like I said, it's only been six months."

Nurse: "It could be fun. You could meet a lot of nice guys. It'd get you out of the house."

Me: "Oh, no. That sounds exhausting to me. I'm good."

Nurse: "Aren't you afraid of being alone? Don't you need a man around the house?"

Me: "Well, no. I think I'm doing okay on my own...."

Nurse: "Oh, I would need a man right away. For sure!"

Me: "Yeah... I think that is something you should talk through with your therapist."

While my grief seems to be lasting for-like-ever, some folks don't grieve for very long. If we've lived with an impending loss, our grieving may seem shorter. Perhaps because we did some grieving before the actual death (also see Anticipatory Grief). Some of us experience little grief, or Absent Grief.

A shortened type of grief is *Abbreviated Grief* and can occur when we try to hijack the process in order to shorten it. Sometimes we do this when we attempt to replace the deceased with another relationship.

Think about it: your aging dog dies and you are heartbroken, but two months later you go to the pound and fall in love with a new puppy. Suddenly your tears dry and you're laughing again. This is a form of abbreviated grief.

Replacing your beloved pet could be healthy and adaptive: the previous relationship was probably quite pure. You didn't have arguments with your dog. You didn't have deep intellectual, emotional, and social bonds with your dog.

You didn't raise children with the dog. You didn't compromise with him on how to remodel the kitchen or where to go on vacation. You didn't fight over money or rage over addictions or argue about the in-laws with your dog.

No, you went for walks, you cuddled on the couch. You threw the stick and he brought it back. You loved him simply and purely, and your grief is likely quite simple and pure.

So you say goodbye to your dog and you grieve for a little bit, but then you find this cute new puppy.

Here's the safe thing about getting a puppy to replace Fido. There is no risk to the ego of the new puppy if you use her as a replacement to the previous dog.

Fifi isn't going to bristle when you accidentally call her "Fido." Fifi won't wonder if you loved Fido more than her.

Fifi won't make demands on you to get rid of Fido's favorite chew toys; she won't ask to wear his favorite collar.

Nope. Fifi will be content with whatever love you have to give her. When you talk about how much you miss your first true love, good old dearly-departed Fido, sweet young Fifi will just smile and wag her tail and lick your face.

But what if you are dating (or, wowza, marrying) in order to replace your former spouse? What if dating is a way for you to expedite your grief by distracting you from your pain? The new spouse might not be so open to walking with you in your grief as Fifi is.

Oh, my friend, there is SO much work that needs to be done before you can move into a healthy connection with a new partner.

Developing a new relationship too soon will create a serious risk to you, to the new person, and to your new relationship (not to mention the risk to others who care about you and don't want to see you hurt).

Please heed my warning *especially* if you have children who are grieving a parent. They need to see you grieve their mom or dad in healthy ways to allow them the space to do the same.

Introducing a new person into the mix and expecting the children to accept and love a new person is asking far too much in the early stages of grief. Even if they like the person, it's a huge challenge to see someone else step into the role that was filled by their deceased parent.

Time is so important to allow the emotions to subside. The kids are in enough pain already; adding to their pain by moving on too quickly is terribly unfair to them.

This doesn't mean you will never have another relationship. It just means you must take the time to do this well.

It is wisdom to do your grief work and to find out who you are going to be now, to learn what you want, what you need, and to work out how you will continue to love the person who is gone, before launching in to a new relationship.

Doing the grief work will lay the healthiest of foundations for you and for the person you hope to love in the future.

There isn't a specific timeline for when grief is resolved, and I can't say with any certainty when it is time for you to start dating after the death of a spouse. But general recommendations are that it is unwise to marry or make any other major decisions during the first year of bereavement, at least.

On another note, other unhealthy behaviors you might use as a way to cope with, or expedite, your grief (drinking, drugs, binge eating, cutting, shopping, gambling, etc.) are also ill-advised. You attempt to shorten or escape your grief when the pain feels too frightening, but instead, you end up with two problems: your grief *and* the consequences of these maladaptive coping strategies.

Take a deep breath, confront and stop the maladaptive behavior or addiction, and *then* tackle the beautiful, hard, yet gratifying work of grieving.

Ambiguous Grief

Ambiguous Grief sometimes refers to grieving someone who is still alive, and it can be generalized further to any loss that has no closure. It can include a loss that is difficult to define.

Divorce, dementia, mental illness, job loss, foreclosure, or the death of a dream can lead to ambiguous grief. Abuse, loss of a childhood, and loss of innocence are ambiguous but *very* real losses as well.

These losses are deep and profound, but because they are not defined, they are not directly mourned either. There is little social support because there is no casket.

A year after my son lost his dad, I ran into his best friend's mom at the store. She told me that she and Tate's dad had divorced recently, and they were going to have to move out of the house. When I got home, I asked my son if Tate had said anything to him about the divorce. No. He had no idea.

With divorce, the losses are gradual and some are vague. "I've lost my dad, but he's not really gone. He's just in an apartment across town." But access to him, the daily rituals you shared, his casual presence in your home is absent. The family, a core structure of your life, has vanished – even though the people are all still alive.

But because it is such an ambiguous event, there is little support. The loss is hard and terrifying and jarring, but, rather than the whole community coming out to share in collective sorrow, few people step in to give comfort.

Jamie's father was a verbally abusive alcoholic. He left her mom for another woman when Jamie was twelve, and Jamie hoped her dad would finally be happy and the verbal abuse would end.

But instead, he poured more of his displeasure and criticism onto Jamie whenever they were together. As she moved into adulthood, every encounter with him would be a tirade of his condemnations and complaints about how Jamie had failed him.

As an adult, Jamie realized she needed to set some boundaries around the relationship. Her dad, unhappy about the boundaries, pushed against them. He found ways to punish her; he even refused to attend her wedding.

Jamie finally realized her dad was too toxic to be in relationship at all and cut off all communication with him.

Jamie's dad has never met her husband. He doesn't even know Jamie has a child of her own. She has heard her dad is ill, has lost his hearing and mobility, and is alone and uncared for. But he's driven everyone who could care for him away.

How many losses is Jamie grieving? Too many to count. Too many to even define. Her father is alive but she grieves the loss of him, as well as the losses related to who he is, who he could have been when she was a child, and who he could be in her life today.

Some of her friends are grieving the death of a parent. They get condolences on Facebook and Instagram. People say, "I'm praying for you." They make casseroles and send cards to acknowledge the loss.

Jamie has received no such support through her myriad losses.

Because these losses are difficult to define, they leave her to search for answers to ambiguous questions. The searching, the yearning, the rumination of grief creates cognitive and emotional loops that are hard to extract and lay end to end.

When Jamie thinks about her dad, there is so much pain, so much guilt, so much distress associated with the losses that she finds she copes best by pushing all of it back out of her awareness. She doesn't get a chance to really process through it.

Ambiguous Grief often lingers in the person's life because there is rarely resolution to it. While "closure" is not really a goal in normal grief, closure seems awfully appealing to the person who is experiencing ambiguous losses.

And yet, of all the forms of grief, closure is hardest to attain here (except with professional help).

Anticipatory Grief

My sister-in-law, Suzy, was diagnosed with a malignant tumor that was wrapped tightly around a major artery in her lung. Surgery wasn't a viable option so oncologists blasted it with radiation and chemotherapy.

The tumor shrank and there was a period of reprieve where she returned to work and to her life.

The tumor began to grow again. It metastasized. It spread to the brain. Slowly, excruciatingly, my brother Brad watched his beloved wife die.

After years of battling the cancer, her death was now imminent. For five long months, Brad sat by Suzy's bedside in their living room.

Brad watched her cognitive and physical functions deteriorate. He carried her. He fed her. He gave her sponge baths and talked to her. He played his harmonica. He worked from home. He did nothing else. He sat by her bed and watched Suzy slowly die.

All that time, Brad readied himself for her death. He anticipated it. He knew it was inevitable but didn't know when.

Could he have grieved her death even when she was still alive? Did he do some of the work of grief while he watched and waited for her death?

Anticipatory Grief is just that: grieving while you anticipate the death of a loved one. We often experience it with terminal illness. We definitely experience anticipatory grief when dementia makes our loved one fade away.

Some wonder if anticipatory grief might shorten the duration of grief after the person dies because much of the work of detaching and saying goodbye—those thousands of little losses—are experienced prior to the actual death.

Others aren't convinced that we can grieve in anticipation of a death. How do you prepare for the death when the person is still alive?

Nonetheless, knowing death will come allows us to say the things we need to say: "I love you," "I'm sorry," "Please forgive me," "Thank you" (the Hawaiian message of ho'oponopono).

It allows us to say, "Goodbye."

Collective Grief

I completed my doctoral internship at the University of Minnesota, Duluth (UMD) where I conducted neuropsychological examinations through their medical school.

One morning I was running a bit late for my first appointment, so I hadn't turned on the television or the radio until halfway into my commute.

When I finally tuned in to the radio, the radio announcer gently informed me that the World Trade Center had been attacked by airplanes; the first plane that hit was initially considered accidental but the second plane was clearly intentional.

I looked around me and realized that I was the only vehicle on the highway. I pulled to the side of the road and cried as I listened to the radio announcer awkwardly try to fill the air space with information that he just didn't have.

I pulled back onto the road and slowly drove to campus. The usually bustling waiting room in the clinic was cavernously empty. Staff were standing around the televisions in their scrubs, weeping.

Everything halted that day. No patients showed up for their appointments. No deliveries were brought in. There was no laughter.

Our nation entered a time of *Collective Grief*.

A community will experience collective grief when a school bus is hit by a truck and children die. A tornado rips through a town and the whole town collectively grieves the change in skyline and terrain. The death of Robin Williams caused a collective grief among my colleagues who study and celebrate humor.

I think we all know and recognize this kind of grief because we have shared in so many collective grief reactions.

Complicated Grief

Complicated Grief (also called *Prolonged* or *Persistent* or *Chronic* grief) is a paralysing grief that doesn't subside. It continues over years without moving toward improved functioning.

It's like the pain of that early grief that many of us experience intermittently, but for the person with complicated grief, there's no reprieve. The person resides in a painful loop as they disappear into their grief without relief.

This grief keeps the person hyper-focused on their loved one. He or she might avoid reminders of the death, have problems accepting it, and might become numb, detached, bitter, isolated, anxious, or depressed. The grief is unremitting, debilitating, long-lasting and severe.

Suicidal ideation is a concern in this type of grief because the bereaved person might feel life has no meaning or purpose now that their loved one is gone; they might believe that life isn't worth living.

Please note: If you are thinking about suicide, please talk to someone who can help. You can call 911 for emergency services, or call a suicide hotline. In the United States, you can call the National Suicide Prevention Lifeline at 800-273-TALK (800-273-8255) to talk with a trained counselor.

One form of complicated grief is called *Delayed Grief,* when the person refuses to confront the reality of the loss and it takes years to even begin to confront it.

Finally, a complicated grief reaction might include *Distorted* Grief, when the bereaved person develops odd behaviors as a result of the loss, often involving anger or self-harming behaviors.

There are some groups of people who are at greater risk for developing Complicated Grief. A violent, unexpected death (accident, murder, or suicide) can create a complicated grief reaction. Losing a child is certainly complicated and can lead to complex grief responses.

When the grieving person has limited social support and was dependent or very close to the deceased, this increases risk of Complicated Grief.

Also, a history of childhood trauma, adult depression, anxiety, PTSD, or other life stressors may also increase one's risk of experiencing a complicated grief reaction.

If any of these are familiar to you, or you think you might have complicated grief, please know that there is hope.

You are experiencing this kind of reaction because the person who died (and your relationship with him or her) significantly mattered to you.

Please locate a bereavement counselor or a grief support group near you to begin to work through this. Online search engines can be very helpful in finding them. There are even resources in the appendix in the back of this book. Talking it through with someone you trust is the single most effective strategy for working through grief complications.

Cumulative Grief

Here's an email from a friend:

Dear Melissa,

Sitting at my computer right now, this feels therapeutic, and I expect tears to follow.

I am a person that keeps everything bottled up and I open up to very few people. The difference now is that I have been praying for a long time that the Lord would lead me and help through some tough things I have been through and continue to go through.

A little background about my family. Since the day my siblings and I entered the world my grandparents (Bert and Margaret) have been there for us. My dad worked at the airline and bartended at night. He was gone a lot while I was growing up, but I always felt my mom had this special connection with me.

The one constant in my life was Grandpa Bert and Grandma Margaret. They did so much for us that it was easy to become their caretakers when they grew old.

I became the person in charge of paying bills, balancing the checkbook, taking Grandma to the grocery store, running errands, dealing with funeral arrangements.

My sister took care of medical appointments, cutting the grass, and making sure Grandma made it to her Friday afternoon hair appointment.

Okay, finally getting to the information you actually asked for. Here's when each one died. Notice less than a year passed from the first one to the last one.

Uncle Bob	*October*
Grandpa (Bert)	*December*
Mom	*January*
Grandma Martin	*January*
Grandma (Margaret)	*July*

Last month my Dad passed away. I regret that I didn't reconnect with him after my grandma's funeral. He left the funeral upset and we didn't speak after that. This is one of my current "you should have" moments. I wish I could have told him, "I forgive you."

Melissa, I know this is way more than you ever thought you would hear from me, but I think maybe God was hoping I would open up a little bit, and you're the one He brought to me.

Thank you,
Lynn

This, my friend, is an example of *Cumulative Grief*. This grief occurs when our grief is intensified by further deaths or multiple losses. The adults Lynn was closest to throughout her life died within a year of each other. If you've stood at the edge of the ocean when waves unpredictably crash against you and threaten to knock you off balance, you have a sense of Lynn's experience.

Rather than having the room and time to process each loss, perhaps addressing each one, the grief compiles. A new loss obscures the last, and the grief process grows complicated. Another response may be that, because it feels so overwhelming, the grief process is halted altogether.

Lynn's grief counselor could ask her how she might set aside time and space to work through each loss. Perhaps a support group would invite her to talk about each person. She'd be wise to press in to the pain of each, individual loss.

Lynn loved each person uniquely. Each relationship was special. So each grief will be unique and special, as well. Each person and relationship requires sufficient attention in the grief process.

Disenfranchised Grief

Phillip was a professional classical bassist in Los Angeles with an impressive resume. He was large and handsome and strong.

But in late 1989, Phillip wasted away, and his mother sadly told her family and friends that he had died of pneumonia.

Yes, he did die of pneumonia, brought on by AIDS. But Loraine was so embarrassed by his actual diagnosis she couldn't speak of it.

Due to the culture of the time, her generation's biases against homosexuality, and the myths around AIDS, Phillip's mother was ashamed that he was a gay man and that he had contracted the virus.

Her shame stopped her from talking about his death, and, consequently, it stopped her from talking about him, her sweet Phillip, her beloved baby boy.

Disenfranchised Grief occurs when we lack the support we need because of the circumstances surrounding the loss. Death by suicide or drug overdose can lead the survivors to feel disenfranchised.

Sometimes we experience disenfranchised grief when we think our grief is insignificant. It's a huge loss to us, but perhaps those around us don't know why the loss matters.

Our pet dies but our extended family diminishes the loss saying, "It was just an animal." Our ex-spouse dies and our friends say, "You divorced him. Why are you sad now?" Your mother-in-law dies and, while she was more like a mother to you, people make "mother-in-law" jokes that sting.

We also see Disenfranchised Grief when the person is mentally or emotionally gone but still alive (due to dementia, mental illness, substance abuse or addiction) and others say, "You're lucky you still have them with you." But you don't feel *lucky* at all.

In my grief group, Linda was grieving her brother's death. Whenever she mentioned him, she would quickly start to hyperventilate, choke on her tears, clench her lips shut to stop herself from speaking, and then blurt out words through heavy gasping sobs.

She would often apologize, saying, "I know he was *just* my brother. I know I shouldn't be grieving this hard."

This already looked like a Disenfranchised Grief because she felt that a death of a sibling wasn't as significant a loss as a spouse's or a child's death.

During the fourth week of the support group, we had ended for the evening, and three of us lingered, standing around the coffee maker, sipping our decaf, eating the last of the mini cupcakes. Linda was haltingly talking about her brother.

And then she said the word, "Suicide."

She dropped her empty paper cup to the ground as she clapped both hands over her mouth. She looked at us, wide-eyed and horrified that she'd said the word. She looked around the room to make sure nobody else had overheard and then fervently apologized, begging us to NEVER share that information with anyone.

Because she'd already said it, though, my friend and I gently lowered ourselves into the nearest chairs and waited for her to continue.

Bill had caused his own death. He had a son in middle school who was *never* to know the real truth about his dad's death. Nobody in the family was allowed to talk about Bill, to discuss his death, or even to remember him aloud due to the risk of the truth coming out.

Now, keep in mind, we all have the freedom to share - and withhold - any information we choose regarding our grief. If you have a loss that you choose not to talk about, this is your right. You do not have to disclose details of a death unless it would help you to talk it through. Your story always belongs to you.

But Linda *needed* to talk about her brother and his death, and should have been able to do so in a supportive group context where confidentiality was respected and fiercely protected. This is the value of a support group.

But, instead, she felt forced to keep quiet. This, my dear friend, was a deeply Disenfranchised Grief.

The death of a pet, the loss of a person we weren't supposed to love, a death by suicide, a lethal drug overdose, a murder within a questionable context, the death of a partner during an extramarital affair: Disenfranchised Grief is the grief we can't talk about it.

So the pain builds and builds without release.

Normal Grief

I know, I know, I started out by saying we don't really know what "normal" is. But we kinda do. I mean, there are some common themes or guidelines.

You'll see what I mean in a minute.

Why am I'm bringing it up now? Well, I'm going through the types of grief alphabetically, and we've reached "N" for "Normal!"

Normal (or Typical) Grief can last from a few months to quite a few years. The Diagnostic and Statistical Manual, Fifth Edition (DSM-5) has suggested "Persistent Complex Bereavement Disorder" may be an upcoming diagnosis if a complex set of symptoms continue after the one-year anniversary of the death.

Frankly, I think we need a different timeline.

My grad school professor told us, "Allow one month of grief for every year of relationship" before diagnosing it as pathological.

If the couple was together for thirty years, and one dies, that's potentially thirty months of active grief. I find this equation helpful. It allows us permission to take it slow.

Such an equation doesn't apply to parents grieving the death of a child. There's no timeline that can predict that trajectory of grief.

What this one-month-for-each-year equation tells us is that Normal Grief can take a really long time for some of us. This equation tells us it takes as long as it needs to take.

Of course, in Normal Grief, there are some shared symptoms like numbness and shock, disbelief, sadness, anxiety around being separated from the loved one.

Almost every person who grieves will cry, have dreams about the loved one, yearn and search for the deceased, feel angry or irritable, and experience other kinds of emotional distress related to the loss.

A rarely talked-about emotion is relief. We feel relief that the suffering is over or that the conflicted relationship has ended. And, unless the relationship was perfect (and perfect relationships are exceedingly rare), almost every one of us will feel guilt over things we said or didn't say, the things we did or failed to do. These are all quite common grief experiences.

Grief has physical symptoms, as well. It can feel like depression or anxiety. Fatigue is very common to mourners and can last for a very long time. The stomach might get involved in the grief: feeling hollow, pained, with either no appetite or a voracious appetite.

In grief, the chest and throat might feel tight and constricted. There is sometimes a nervousness or agitation where the person can't feel settled or relaxed. These are common symptoms.

There will also likely be grief bursts, when the person has brief periods (20-30 minutes, for example) of intense emotion. These bursts might be prompted by a reminder or trigger, and often the person feels ambushed by the intensity of the grief reaction.

Sometimes these grief bursts are called "grief pangs"; a "pang" being a sudden and sharp spasm of emotion, sometimes described as a stab or shooting pain. Grief pangs; isn't that a fantastic, perfectly descriptive phrase?

There are thoughts that are common to grief, as well. We often begin with disbelief; we can't believe it happened. It makes no sense that they're really gone. We feel confused. We can't concentrate or focus on anything for very long.

When I was first grieving my husband's death, my friend would give others updates on how I was doing: "Well," she would say, "she can focus on something for about ninety seconds now."

As I progressed through those first few months, she would cheerfully update them and say, "She's doing better. Now she can concentrate for about five minutes."

Some of us become preoccupied with the deceased. We think about them all the time. The thoughts might be intrusive and unwanted. The deceased is constantly on our mind and we can't seem to think or talk about anything else.

Sometimes we ruminate on the death or on a specific encounter we had with them or on something we did wrong in the relationship. This is normal.

A few of us have the sensation that the person is present with us. We might see them, hear them, or feel we are being watched. Some grief specialists would explain this experience (that our loved one is near) during waking hours as a form of hallucination.

No matter what explanation we give it, the presence of the deceased can range from comforting to frightening.

Grief can include all kinds of behaviors—all performed to meet a need for connection. A wife becomes an avid football fan after her husband died so she can connect with him through a shared love for the team. For years, a child sleeps with his mom's nightgown as his pillowcase so he can feel closer to her as he falls asleep. The widow routinely dips her fingers in her husband's ashes and licks them.

The behaviors we engage in to feel closer to the deceased do not necessarily define the normalcy of our grief. Our behaviors might seem odd or even distressing. But the *desire* to connect with the deceased, no matter how we try to do it, is normal.

The primary feature of Normal Grief is movement toward resolution. Slowly, the person experiences fewer symptoms, with less frequency, lower intensity, and with a gradual approach toward acceptance of the loss.

All the other types of grief I describe in this chapter seem to reflect some kind of obstacle that prevents the mourner from reaching resolution.

Stay with me. We will get to a place in this book where we can accomplish resolution by setting goals and finding meaning.

Secondary Grief

I never realized how much my husband, Scott, did for our family until he died. Don't get me wrong, I was always quick to show my gratitude and would continually thank him for his hard work. But the full reality of his contributions hadn't really hit until he was gone.

Bear with me as I list what he did: Scott bought all of our groceries. He cooked all the meals, took care of our vehicles, and managed our finances. He bought all gifts, all the cards, planned the parties. He was a primary caregiver to our children. He contributed more than half of our income but he also brought the garbage down to the end of the driveway on Tuesday nights.

In the cold Minnesota winters, he cleared the snow, and in the hot summers he'd grill our suppers. He'd take the kids sledding and golfing and horseback riding; he attended all the 4-H events and band concerts. (Holy buckets. No wonder the guy was tired.)

This is only the tip of the iceberg of what Scott contributed to my life. I can't even begin to identify the depth of emotional support he gave me. The love and tenderness and affection that died when he went away.

Now I am parenting two teenagers who are grieving the death of their really good dad. He poured out every measure of energy and affection onto them. He loved them with such beautiful ferocity, it was visible and tangible. Now his love feels absent to them.

I see their grief and it causes me to grieve the end of their innocence. I grieve the loss of their security, their dashed expectations to have their dad at their graduations and weddings, their shaken belief in a just world, their serious questions about a good and loving God, and on and on and on.

This grief lays on top of the thousands of other losses I have experienced because he died. These layers, my friend, reveal secondary losses.

This is *Secondary Grief.*

Traumatic Grief
When a death is abrupt, violent, and/or unexpected, the grief might be *Traumatic Grief.*

There are a number of other reasons the grief may be considered traumatic: if your loved one was mutilated, if they suffered prior to the death (from painful illness to torture), if the death was unnatural, preventable, intentional, or random.

If there were a number of people who died at the same time, or if you, the bereaved, witnessed the death, this can also cause Traumatic Grief.

Separate, but definitely traumatic, is the death of one's child. No matter the age or cause of death, the death of a child can result in what we would label as Traumatic Grief.

Regardless of the cause, Traumatic Grief is difficult to navigate because of intrusive thoughts, images, disturbing or recurring nightmares. Your previously controlled and sheltered world is shattered; your sense of safety is violated.

In Traumatic Grief, your mind doesn't seem to work the way it should. You can't think straight. Perhaps you are on edge, irritable; you overreact to things, and maybe make decisions you later regret.

When my mother was killed in the car crash, a few of my siblings and I went to the scene of the accident. We saw the shattered glass glittering in the sun, sprinkled through the ditch grass. We saw the black rubber stripes stained diagonally across the tar of the highway where brakes had been applied and locked up.

Her van was in the ditch. It was almost unrecognizable; no longer shaped like a van. The driver's side was curled around an invisible semi bumper.

The grass around the van was trampled where first responders raced to rescue her but failed.

Her purse was still on the floor where it had been tossed, a piece of half-eaten toast in a napkin was tucked in the fold of the passenger seat, an empty coffee cup still in the cup holder.

Even now, so many years later, I can see these images when I close my eyes. They show up in my dreams, unwanted. They startle me awake.

I wish I had never looked.

Traumatic Grief can look an awful lot like Post Traumatic Stress Disorder (PTSD).

Symptoms may include anguish around the memories of the death, upsetting dreams or nightmares about the death, intrusive re-experiencing of the event, feeling numb and detached from others, having a hard time concentrating or working, irritability, socially pulling away from others, insomnia, and constantly scanning your environment looking for other threats. These are symptoms of both PTSD and Traumatic Grief. These are sources of serious distress.

If you see yourself in this kind of grief, please seek help. Effective treatments are being developed for the treatment of PTSD.

Grief is difficult enough, my dear reader. Adding a layer of trauma can make it virtually un-endurable. There is no shame in having this kind of reaction, and treatment is available.

If you are a veteran, there is a Veterans Crisis Line: 1-800-273-8255 (press 1). If you are not a veteran, there are mental health treatment referral helplines available. For example, the Substance Abuse and Mental Health Services Administration (SAMHSA) has a helpline at 1-800-622- HELP (4357).

Please see the appendix with resources for additional online and face-to-face support groups and therapies.

Treating trauma is a mental health issue just like treating your acid reflux is a physical health issue or wearing glasses is an eye health issue. All of these are basic health issues. No stigma. No shame.

Please, get help.

Unresolved Grief

Sometimes grief just won't resolve.

In relationships that were less than perfect, we linger in the pain that we felt when they were alive.

If we fought a lot, for example, we may linger in our regret, constantly coming back to our struggle with the person.

We have a hard time moving through our grief because of the difficulty in the relationship. It's a challenge to find resolution. We can't go back and make things right. We can't restore the relationship.

Faith and Hope were cute, blonde fraternal twins, born only a few minutes apart.

Faith learned to walk and talk quickly, while Hope struggled to crawl and pull herself up.

Faith taught herself to read while Hope was still learning her alphabet.

Faith excelled in school, but Hope required special services.

Faith dated and was voted homecoming queen. Hope was never asked out by a boy.

When Faith received welcome packets and scholarship offers from universities, Hope was struggling to graduate high school.

Faith was athletic: healthy and robust. Hope was chronically ill and constantly in pain.

When the girls were in their early twenties, their mother, Tammy, received a phone call telling her that Hope had died from a sudden onset asthma attack at work.

Twenty years later, when asked if she still missed Hope, Tammy divulged, "Life didn't come easy to Hope, and that made life hard for us."

Because of the many obstacles Hope faced, and the constant self-comparison to her twin, she was pessimistic, ill-tempered, and often angry.

Tammy admits that grieving was a challenge because of all of the pain that she endured when she watched Hope struggle.

It was also hard to grieve her loss because of the pain she felt when Hope lashed out at her.

What makes a person "difficult" and thereby difficult to grieve? So many factors: mental health issues, emotional problems, addictions, disability, dementia.

Not all of us lived with an abuser or an addict. More of us lived with a person who was just... flawed. They were critical of you, impatient with the kids, easily irritated with others, or blaming everyone for their unhappiness. Maybe they were a bully or a fault-finder.

Then they went and died.

No matter the conditions or the personality dispositions that made them difficult, the reality is that they *were* difficult, and now we, the survivors, are stuck agonizing over how hard it was to love them sometimes.

If you're like me, you feel guilty because you didn't love them enough.

As a psychotherapist, my mind almost immediately goes to the challenges of mental illness that create trauma in relationships.

Mental illness is a sickness. Instead of affecting our physical functioning, mental illness impacts our psychological, emotional, behavioral and relational functioning.

Like any illness, we don't want it, we can't control it, and the demands of finding a medication and/or treatment for it can overwhelm us and play into the despair around the illness.

I compare it to my very embarrassing autoimmune disorder. I have Ulcerative Colitis, which is a syndrome where the immune system identifies the colon as a foreign body, and attacks to destroy it. The colon becomes inflamed, ulcerated, and damaged. It bleeds, it oozes, it scars (I know, I know, too much information. Sorry).

As a result of this disease, though, I face horrible, uncontrolled and unmanageable symptoms. My disease has been a prison for me. For years, I had no control over the symptoms: the pain, the urgency, the bloating, the bleeding, any of it.

Medications didn't seem to touch the symptoms, and I thought my life would be forever controlled by this disease. Fortunately, through persistence, I finally found a doctor who could help me with the right medication that has put me in remission.

There is a reason I'm telling you this. A mental illness shares very similar themes: serious symptoms, feelings of distress, experiences of being trapped by it, struggles to find a way to manage it that works, loss of hope that it will ever go away. We have to be persistent in finding the right doctor and the right treatments.

Some examples of mental illness include depression and bipolar disorders, anxiety, panic disorder, eating disorders, schizophrenia, and substance use disorders (like alcoholism and other addictions).

Having one of these mental health issues creates serious distress. The person with the disorder desperately wants their depression to lift, their anxiety to subside, their focus and attention to improve.

As much as you complain and cry about a loved one's addiction, they are in even greater distress because they are imprisoned by it and feel unable to break out.

More serious and persistent mental illnesses, like schizophrenia, dissociative disorders, or dementia might remove the person from us and leave their shell behind.

These are difficult illnesses for the person to suffer, and we hurt watching them. Sometimes we get frustrated because we think they could have tried harder to fight the disease. We wish they had been more diligent at finding a treatment.

When your loved one was well, they were wonderful. When they were sick, everyone seemed to suffer.

Maybe it was hard to tell where they began and the disease ended—what part was really them and what part was the disorder?

Please, my beloved reader, do not lose sight of the fact that mental illness can hurt both the person who has the illness and your relationship with them.

As you grieve and look back over your relationship, you may have to unpack your role in it, but also the role of the mental illness in their functioning.

Be clear that the behavior wasn't always a reflection of them or their character. Perhaps their behavior was a symptom of illness.

You may know very well how difficult it was to separate the person from their disease. In Unresolved Grief, we can't reconcile it. We carry the struggles, the symptoms, and our conflicted encounters into our grief. We spin around and around, grieving and crying and remembering the hard parts, not able to make sense of it, and not able to resolve our grief and bring it to a peaceful conclusion.

Please see the Resource List in the back of the book. Finding support from a mental health professional or a support group might help you step outside of your grief cycle. It is important you seek help to gain clarity and move toward resolution.

Now that I've discussed the types of grief, you might wonder what we can do with this information. Are we passive participants, bearing witness to our own grief but unable to do anything about it?

Or is there something we can do to move forward?

What do I do with my pain? Is there a purpose to it? Is there relief?

Tasks of Grief

When I studied for my master's thesis on patterns, processes, and obstacles of bereavement, there weren't a lot of theories out there on how to navigate the grief process.

Early theorists opened up the dialog of grief, and some of the later theorists further helped us understand what we need to accomplish in our grief process. These theorists have tried to explain how we might resolve our grief and find peaceful resolution.

They all use some pretty complex language. Don't worry. I'll translate, and I'll try to keep you awake.

In this next section we will look at some of the historical and current grief theories and we will review the most current practices in grief work.

As dry as this sounds, though, you are actually going to come away with new ways of thinking about grief. I hope you find things to do today in your grief process.

Freud

I am sorry to begin this section with words that may seem unkind. But usually when I read *Freud*, I often hear a voice in the back of my head that says, "This guy was a nut."

While he was a father of psychology, and he was the first to really think about the internal workings of the mind, most of what he proposed is not scientifically supported. His was a brilliant mind, yes, but we have progressed so far beyond most of the theories he developed.

Yet it is necessary for me to start at the beginning with some historical antecedents to current grief theories. That means I begin with Freud.

Even with all of my criticisms, I'm quite happy to admit that his writings on Mourning (grief) aren't too far off.

Attaboy, Sigmund.

As part of his "Collected Papers" (1917), Freud wrote an article called "Mourning and Melancholia" (isn't that quite the throwback title? If you saw it on the shelves of Barnes and Noble, I'm guessing you wouldn't rush to grab it off the shelf before the lady next to you could reach for it).

On Mourning and Melancholia, Freud writes:

> *Mourning is regularly the reaction to the loss of a loved person, or to the loss of some abstraction which has taken the place of one, such as fatherland, liberty, and ideal, and so on. As an effect of the same influences, melancholia instead of a state of grief develops in some people, whom we consequently suspect of a morbid pathological disposition. It is also well worth notice that, although grief involves grave departures from the normal attitude to life, it never occurs to us to regard it as a morbid condition and hand of the mourner over to medical treatment. We rest assured that after a lapse of time it will be overcome, and we can look upon any interference with it as inadvisable or even harmful* (Freud, 1917, p. 153).

What the heck, you say? Fuzzy writing, you say? Hard to understand, you say?

Just think, this was *after* translation from German to English.

Allow me to translate a little further: Freud is saying that mourning (grief) and melancholia (depression) are different.

Grief is not a disorder but is a natural reaction to loss. He believes it is not pathological, and I agree. Grief is not a sickness. We don't need to seek medical treatment, and it will resolve over time, allowing us to return to our normal life.

Melancholia, or clinical depression, however, *is* an illness. It is dysfunctional, distressing, and potentially dangerous. It deviates from the norm (most people don't experience crippling depression); it prohibits us from functioning in the important areas of our lives (we shut down and can't work, study, parent, or feel joy).

Depression is distressing because it overwhelms our basic ability to cope with life, and it is dangerous if the person considers suicide as the only solution to the pain.

Because it is deviant, dysfunctional, distressing, and dangerous, depression is a form of pathology; illness.

While grief and depression may look an awful lot alike, there are some distinct differences and similarities that Freud (1917) describes. For example, in depression there is dejection, pulling away from activities, sadness, isolation. We see these in grief as well.

But in depression, there is also self-reproach, self-loathing, an expectation of punishment, and low self-esteem. We don't tend to experience those self-criticisms as much in grief.

One can experience depression as a result of the death of a loved one. The pronounced difference between grief and depression is this: in grief, we know what we've lost, and in depression, we aren't quite sure.

The pronounced similarity between grief and depression is this: both involve the absorbing work of sadness and loss of a loved one. In grief, the loved one is another person. In depression, the lost loved one is the self.

Here's how Freud (1917) describes the exhausting nature of grief:

> *This [grief] struggle can be so intense that a turning away from reality ensues.... The normal outcome is that deference for reality gains the day. Nevertheless its behest cannot be at once obeyed. The task is now carried through bit by bit, under great expense of time and cathectic energy, while all the time the existence of a lost object is continued in the mind. It is worth noting that this pain seems natural to us (p. 154).*

In other words, we cling to our deceased loved one. We dream of them; we long for them; we wish for them the return to us.

But reality overtakes us, even when we want to stay in relationship with the deceased. So, bit by bit, we sift through each memory and slowly detach from the grief as we move through the process.

I think Freud really nails it on this part. This is *exactly* my experience. My dad appears in my dreams. I see my mother in crowds and across the street. I often see people who remind me of the friends I've lost. I search for my husband.

When my mom died, I was drawn to women with her haircut. I wanted women her age to step in and be a mother to me. I went through photographs and studied her face. I retold stories about her, about us, to anyone who would listen. Each memory, each story told, was a release of my grief.

So Freud was on to something in identifying the differences between depression and grief and describing how grief slowly lifts as we search for our loved one and sift through the memories, ever so slowly detaching from the intensity of emotion.

Lindeman's Symptoms and Tasks

In the 1940s, psychiatrist Erich Lindemann, studied grief. He developed not only a set of symptoms common to bereavement but also some "work" one must do to resolve one's grief. I think he was on to something, even if the language he used was sometimes less than desirable.

"What do you mean, Dr. Mork?" you ask.

Just wait. You'll see.

Symptoms:

Lindemann (1944) believed the common symptoms of bereavement included physical distress. This is a loss of appetite, insomnia, low energy, fatigue, loss of motivation.

I wish I had a loss of appetite. My grief makes me cavernously hungry. So I'm grieving—and battling my weight. Lucky me.

Another symptom of grief, according to Lindemann, is a preoccupation with images of the person who is gone.

I mean, of course. We think about them. We study photos of them in different outfits, different expressions, in various contexts, at different angles. We gaze at pictures and notice how cute he was in that jacket. How gorgeous his smile. How great he looked when his hair curled out under his baseball cap; how good he looked in his jeans....

Or is it just me that does that?

Lindemann also identified guilt as a prominent symptom of grief.

Wowza, he nailed this one too. I couldn't stop dwelling on the failures I'd committed in our marriage. When I'd been petulant. When I'd not apologized. When I'd yelled and complained and withheld affection. So many failures, with heavy guilt attached to each.

Hostile reactions were another symptom Lindemann named, where we are just so easily frustrated or irritated by others. Perhaps anger, irritability, and hostility are symptoms we don't realize are as common to grief as they are.

Along with hostility, there is a "loss of pattern of conduct." Odd language, right?

But what it means is that basic activities or tasks overwhelm us. Simple decisions are taxing. Cooking dinner is a serious chore. We step out of the shower and realize we hadn't actually washed anything. Work tasks can be paralyzing.

Eileen is one of the sweetest women you'll ever meet. She's the kind of grandmotherly lady who keeps cookies in the freezer in the event someone might stop by and be in desperate need of a ginger snap.

But when her husband died, she manifested a few of these symptoms that Lindemann describes. She suffered a "loss of pattern of conduct."

At the grocery store, when asked by the clerk to choose paper or plastic, Eileen acted as though she were being asked to make Sophie's Choice. She hissed at the clerk, "I don't know. My *husband* died."

It makes sense, though. Grief takes up so much cognitive and emotional space. There is little margin to tolerate much else. Minor irritations or inconveniences feel intolerable because we just don't have the ability to manage them when our minds are so busy with our grief.

The last grief reaction Lindemann describes is an adoption of the traits of the person who has died. You might embrace an interest or hobby they loved, you might start walking like them, or even see some resemblance of them when you look in the mirror. When I wash my hands, I see my mother's hands fluttering under the stream of tap water. My daughter wears her dad's navy-blue cardigan when she travels as a way to bring him with her.

Lindemann's Grief Work

When my clients come to me asking for help with their grief, they are not asking me to describe the stages they might be passively moving through.

They come to me because they want to know what they need to *do*. They feel stuck. They are afraid the pain will never remit. They are frightened by the intensity of the feelings they have and want to know how to confront them (or more commonly, escape them). But they are also desperate to hold on to the person who's died.

So Lindemann was wise to identify some fairly common symptoms of grief, but he also identified some tasks of "grief work."

I think Lindemann was the first theorist who argued that we didn't have to be passive participants in the process, riding along on our waves of grief, hoping to eventually land on the other side. Nope. Lindemann said there is grief work to be done, and three tasks through which we can do it.

The first task was **"emancipation from bondage to the deceased."** (I told you at the beginning of this section that his language was weird.)

Let me say that, while I really like that he came up with tasks to accomplish, I already take issue. This is a potentially problematic task, not only because of the language he uses, but because of what he wants us to accomplish here.

What he is proposing is that we find a way to let go of the deceased. Sadly, this first task is precisely what many of us want to avoid. I certainly don't want to be released from my attachment to my parents, my friends, the babies I've lost, or my husband. They are all too much a part of my life, my story, my identity.

As I was preparing to speak at a grief coalition one evening, setting my notes on the podium, a woman came up to me. She introduced herself and explained that her young daughter had died a year before.

The woman told me that she'd read a lot of books and heard a lot of speakers on the topic of grief and was looking forward to hearing what I had to share.

Then she leaned in and softly warned me, "If you tell us that we need to find closure, say goodbye to our loved one, or, God-forbid, tell us to 'gently close the lid on the casket,' I will walk right up here while you are still mid-sentence, and I will personally slap you across the face."

Then she warmly smiled at me, gently patted my hand, and returned to her seat.

Nope. She did not want emancipation.

The second task, according to Lindemann (1944), is **"readjustment to a new environment in which the deceased is missing."** This is a task that appears in other theories as well, and I do see some value in this.

This loss is a reality that must be faced—my house will never again feel Scott's footsteps. My bed will not sag under his weight. The toothbrush that stands at attention in the cup will never again clean his teeth. A new photo of him will never be taken. There are no new jokes to share. These are all horrible realities I have to confront and accept.

Lindemann's task, then, is to slowly adjust to this new life.

Finally, the third task is **"the formation of new relationships."** In order to do this, Lindemann says we need to accomplish the first two tasks by letting go of the bond we have with the person who is gone.

This is a delicate topic for some of us. As a young, grieving parent, this is akin to hearing "Well, at least you can have another baby!"

I don't want another baby. I wanted *this* baby.

Lindemann held the 1940's perspective that relationships might be replaced. But they can't. And they don't need to be.

A child who has died is still our child. Our hearts burst with love that needs to be poured out onto her. That love is meant only for her; can only be directed onto her.

There may come a day when our focus can broaden to others; perhaps someday we can look at other people's children and feel joy. And certainly, as a new baby grows in our body, love for that new baby grows in our heart. But do not let anyone tell you to set a goal of replacing the child who has died.

But what about those who are widowed? Some might feel alone and lonely and curious if they can be in another relationship.

A client asked me once, "Am I unfaithful to my husband if I start dating again? Can I love more than one person at a time? Do I have to stop loving my dead spouse?"

This is a question I think many grieving spouses ask. I can't imagine having to sever my connection to my husband. Death didn't kill my love for him. Does that mean I will live a life of singleness because there's only room for love of one man in my heart?

It's strange, because we don't ask that about other relationships. Can I love more than one friend at a time, or can I make room for all of them? Can I love more than one child at a time?

Of course.

I didn't stop grieving the lost pregnancies when we had our first live birth. I didn't have to relinquish my love for my daughter when my son was born.

I have six brothers—all whom I love with deep tenderness. They are all different; so uniquely themselves. Six big loving men in my life, these brothers, and each one seems to hold my whole heart in his big, gentle hands.

Klass, Silverman, and Nickman (1996) write:

"...it is clear in practical experience that to care, to be involved in more than one relationship at a time, is part of the human condition whether the other people in the relationship are present, absent, or dead. To insist on a separateness that keeps very clear boundaries between people requires a mechanistic view of human functioning that fails to appreciate the importance of connection and relationship" (p.14).

Agreed. We aren't machines. Connection and relationship are too precious to assume we can just cut off one for the sake of beginning a new one.

Do we have to sever our attachment to the person who is gone in order to forge a new relationship? No, Dr. Lindemann, I don't believe we do.

Lindemann (1944) moved the field forward in providing a theory of grief stages, and it was valuable insight for the time. However, current research and anecdotal evidence shows he was a little off the mark.

There's much more to consider before we have a congruent and holistic view of grief work. As we move forward in this chapter, we will explore more facets of this process.

Kubler-Ross' Stages of Grief

While most people know who Freud is, most are surprised to know that he wrote about mourning. Unless one has studied grief theory, one likely does not know about Lindemann.

However, when a layperson outside the field of grief work is asked for a name associated with grief studies, most will name Kubler-Ross's (1973) and her stages of grief.

When I mentioned to a friend over dinner once that I would be writing some thoughts about grief, she narrowed her eyes, leaned forward, and demanded to know, "What do you think about Kubler-Ross's stages of grief?"

I answered, "I think she's brilliant, but I don't think her stages were meant to describe bereavement work."

She clapped her hands together, leaned back, and said, "Thank you."

Before one can criticize Kubler-Ross, it's important to *read* Kubler-Ross. If you haven't read her book, "On Death and Dying" (1973), please do. It is a beautifully written book that opens wide the hidden beauty of death that we too often disguise, anesthetize, euthanize, or enshroud.

In her book, Kubler-Ross lays bare what happens to a society when we hide away from death. She takes the medical community to task for attempting to shield the very patients who are dying from the reality of their impending death. She cautions physicians to shift from "Should we tell...?" to "How do we tell...?" During the time of her writing, this was a significant paradigm shift in the medical community.

When I reflect on Scott's illness, I recall how devastating it was to not know his prognosis. There were a few weeks between knowing he had a tumor—to knowing what kind of tumor it was—to knowing how much it had spread. The ambiguity, the *not* knowing, was agonizing and torturous.

In April, we learned he had a malignant tumor in his lung.

In May, they said new treatments could give him years.

In June, they gave him maybe a year.

In July, they gave him months.

In August, they gave him weeks.

On September 1st they gave him hours.

He died that evening.

Within four and a half months they went from telling us he had years to telling me he had hours.

Each time they changed his prognosis, my heart broke again, but I also felt more peace in knowing I could trust them to tell me the truth as they discovered it. Kubler-Ross (1973) deserves credit for forcing this honesty in medicine and terminal diagnosis.

When Kubler-Ross (1973) discusses the actual stages of grief, she is talking about the dying patients she and her student researchers interviewed. She found that there were themes that emerged regarding ways they processed the information: "[this] is an attempt to summarize what we have learned from our dying patients in terms of coping mechanisms at the time of a terminal illness (Kubler-Ross, 1973, p. 31)."

Remember this. She is discussing the stages as *coping mechanisms*—default strategies we use to manage unbearable stress. Also, even though she didn't research bereavement, these stages hold great similarity to what we experience in our bereavement process.

As we read through, where do you find yourself residing right now in your own grief?

First Stage: Denial

This first stage of denial is the "Nope, not me. This can't be happening to me" stage. Sometimes it's managed by believing the tests results are wrong. That the doctors are confused. That the prognosis isn't that bad. That others have been healed of this disease and so can I.

These stages are all healthy, by the way. None of the stages are maladaptive or wrong. Denial, for example, is a very healthy (and slow) adaptation to the truth.

We manage to see some things most clearly when we can view them at arms' length. When the thing gets too close, our view is obscured.

Think about a poster on a wall. If you view it from a distance, you see it clearly. If you attempt to read it with your nose pressed against the poster, it can't be read clearly.

Our use of denial is a way of slowly acquainting ourselves with the writing on wall, so to speak.

Kubler-Ross (1973) allows that this can be a fleeting stage— that some people respond to the news of their terminal illness with shock and then rebound to address the reality of the illness—while others stay in this place of shock and denial for extended periods of time. They isolate themselves from others; pulling away while they attempt to make sense of the prognosis.

Second Stage: Anger

So the first stage inevitably wears off, and the person begins to adapt to the reality of the prognosis. Then they are *livid.*

It's not just the disease that receives the ire. Anger shoots out sideways at anyone within range: The doctors are morons. The nurses are inattentive. The hospice folks are neglectful. The neighbors, who have smoked their entire adult lives, deserve this lung cancer, not my sweet, diet-coke drinking, Jesus-loving husband (Can you tell I've identified with this stage?).

When the doctors refused to put Scott on hospice because there were treatments they believed could be helpful, I was so relieved to know there was still some hope.

To me, hospice meant end-stage cancer and end-of-life care. It meant giving up on possible treatments and letting him die peacefully.

I wasn't ready to put Scott on hospice. No, the doctors said. We aren't there yet. There are treatments left to try.

Instead, they sent out a palliative care aide to assist with basic care-giving tasks like trimming his nails and massaging his legs.

When she arrived, she spent *a lot* of time showering our dog with affection and then talking about her own dogs and how precious they were.

Whatever. Fine. Can we talk about Scott, though?

Then she began running through an assessment worksheet, asking Scott about his pain levels and his difficulties in functioning.

As he reviewed his serious concerns with her, she casually mentioned that perhaps we should consider hospice.

She said his pain levels were so high and his symptoms so distressing, hospice could help him. Perhaps, she said, he should forego all future cancer treatments. Allow the cancer to take its course, she said. At least in hospice he would be comfortable, she said. It's time to accept that death from this cancer was inevitable, she said.

Oh.

No.

Please believe me when I tell you that I don't use the F-bomb. I have quite a large vocabulary and generally rely on it to communicate clearly. I don't really need cuss words as sentence enhancers.

But all I could do was swear at her. I've never cussed so much in my entire life as I did in that stream of insults pouring out of my mouth! Even the cats seemed to cover their ears.

I stood over this poor woman who was sitting at my kitchen table, petting my dog and drinking my coffee, and I told her she was an effen-terrible person and effing-bad at her job. Who the F did she think she was, telling my husband to give in to his flipping cancer? I told her to get the effenheimer out of my house and to never F-bomb darken my door again.

Then I icily stared her down as she packed up her nursing gear and file folders and tiptoed out of my house.

Do you think I might have been in the "Anger" stage of his terminal illness?

Yes.

Perhaps.

Third Stage: Bargaining

This stage is heartbreaking. Well, they are all heartbreaking. This one is particularly hard.

According to Kubler-Ross:

> The bargaining is really an attempt to postpone; it has to include a prize offered "for good behavior," it also sets a self-imposed "deadline...," and it includes an implicit promise that the patient will not ask for more if this one postponement is granted (1973, p. 720).

When Scott was diagnosed, he looked at me and, with tears in his eyes, said, "I wanted to see who the kids would be when they grew up."

Our boy is a smart, funny, creative kid. He was only twelve years old at the time.

Scott asked the doctors if he'd live to see his son graduate high school. Their reluctant answer was, "Possible, but not likely."

So, Scott bargained with God and the doctors, "Well, then, can I see my daughter graduate?"

She was seventeen; starting her senior year of high school in a few months. Yes, this seemed like a reasonable bargaining request.

Doctors couldn't answer the question because they didn't know how he'd respond to treatment—if there'd be a "stay in his execution," so to speak.

Throughout his short illness, on the white board in the hospital, under family questions, our daughter would write, "Will he live to see me graduate?" She (and we) had subscribed to Scott's bargaining.

When the doctors looked at her as we neared the end of the summer and we approached the start of the new school year, they finally had the answer. "No, honey, he won't see you graduate."

He died on Friday.

School started the following Tuesday. His visitation was Wednesday. His funeral on Thursday. They went back to school again on Friday.

This was the first week of my daughter's senior year and my son's eighth grade.

Bargaining is a coping strategy to deal with the reality of the prognosis. It never actually works to help anybody get more time.

Fourth Stage: Depression

The fourth stage Kubler-Ross identifies is depression. I cannot describe this any more eloquently than Kubler-Ross herself:

> *All these reasons for depressions are well known to everybody who deals with patients. What we often tend to forget, however, is the preparatory grief that the terminally ill patient has to undergo in order to prepare himself for his final separation from this world* (Kubler-Ross, 1973, p. 75).

Kubler-Ross describes two different kinds of depression in the context of death and dying: *Reactive Depression,* where the person is sad about all the losses related to the illness (loss of functioning, loss of strength, loss of relationships as people fall away), and *Preparatory Depression,* where the person is grieving the losses related to the end of life.

Reactive depression is a reaction to past losses, and preparatory depression is taking into account impending losses. The first can be countered with "...yes, that's hard, but look at the bright side. At least I still have...."

The second cannot be countered with anything.

Encouragements and reassurances are meaningless, platitudes are empty, and clichés are painful to hear. So the second kind of depression is a quiet depression:

> *In the preparatory grief there is no or little need for words. It is much more a feeling that can be mutually expressed and is often done better with a touch of a hand, a stroking of the hair or just a silent sitting together* (Kubler-Ross, 1973, p. 77).

This is excellent advice for the helpers in bereavement, as well.

Fifth Stage: Acceptance

After the denial has lifted, the anger has been expressed, bargaining has been negotiated, and the depression has been resolved, the person enters a stage of acceptance.

The person who is dying reaches a place of quiet agreement that this is the end. He or she might sleep more, not as a form of resignation, or hopeless giving up; instead, this stage of acceptance is a period of rest. It is the "'final rest before the long journey'" as described by one of Kubler-Ross' patients (1973, p. 102).

Interest in the outside world diminishes, verbal interactions decrease, and the patient begins to turn inward as they prepare for the end.

Kubler-Ross summarizes the purpose of her book with this: "If this book serves no other purpose but to sensitize family members of terminally ill patients and hospital personnel to the implicit communications of dying patients, then it has fulfilled its task" (1973, p. 129).

You can see from this statement that she had no intention of describing the stages of bereavement after a patient had died. She wasn't describing the stages of mourning that we must navigate. These are stages of adjusting to the reality of one's own impending death and the ways caregivers can understand and assist the process.

Ask me, "What do you think about Kubler-Ross' Stages of Grief?"

I think she's a genius. I just don't think we have used her stages in the way in which she intended.

She described the stages of grief as one prepares to die. However, over the past forty years, many counselors have used her work as the template to understand the bereavement process, as well.

Allow me a brief commentary on the idea of stages in grief. The concept of "stages" implies that we are all processing through very similar patterns of loss, which is true. But the idea of stages also suggests that we are passive observers of our grief.

Sometimes that's true; we are passive observers. We are so overwhelmed by the loss that we can't possibly be intentionally active in the process of grief.

It took grief theorists a long time to come back to the idea that there were some tasks we could accomplish to actively aid us in our grief work.

We will get there. I promise. No need to be so impatient, buddy. First, we need to discuss a few other theorists who attempted to explain bereavement.

Bowlby and Parkes: Four Phases of Grief

John Bowlby (1961) came along shortly after Freud. He was the first person to look at the bonds between mother and child based on observation and research. Every student who has read even the introductory texts of psychology is familiar with John Bowlby's work.

Working for the World Health Organization as a post-war consultant, Bowlby saw the trauma children experienced when they lost their mothers. From observing that trauma, he developed a theory of grief (Bowlby, 1961).

He theorized that there is a strong psychological bond that forms between an infant and a caregiver, and both parent and child work very hard to maintain the bond. Similar attachments form in other relationships: spousal, sibling, friend, etc.

When that bond is broken, there will be psychological trauma including protest, despair, yearning, and detachment (Bowlby, 1961). These were concepts he generalized to grief.

What happens in this grief, then, when the attachment or bond is broken by death? The survivor is left to endure that psychological trauma. Bowlby, with his colleague, Colin Murray Parkes (1970), developed a theory of four stages of grief through which they believed we must all go.

Phase 1: Shock and Numbness

This phase of grief occurs quickly after the death. We are stunned, numb, staring blankly into the void. We are occasionally overcome with sadness or grief bursts, but the primary experience is numbness.

The beauty of this stage is that it allows us to function in the face of the culturally prescribed behaviors that we must do: calling friends and family to notify them of the death, planning or implementing the funeral, making tough decisions about the first weeks of mourning, greeting people, writing thank you cards, and so on.

This numbness and shock even allows us to return to work or school as we dissociate the reality of the loss from the regular demands of our life

Phase 2: Yearning and Searching

Oh, boy, if you have grieved, or are grieving, you *know* this stage. We long for our loved one. We search for them. We ache.

I admit that I am a yearner. I yearn for people, places, relationships, experiences. It's a deep ache in my gut.

I visited the Musee D'Orsay in Paris when I accompanied my daughter on a work trip. There was a painting there that stunned me. It captured a place I'd longed for my whole life but had never visited. I stood there, staring at it, quietly weeping and aching to be there. I was homesick for a place I had never been.

Oh, I am definitely a yearner.

After Scott died, I searched for him everywhere. In crowds, I'd look for someone with his build. I'd call his phone, hoping he'd answer. Then I'd cry when I'd hear his outgoing message.

In my dreams I would even scan imaginary dream-crowds for him. I'd visually walk through the farm, trying to locate where he'd be riding his horse. I pined for him.

It reminds me a little bit of geese.

Worden (2008) writes,

"Ethologist Konrad Lorenz (1963) has described this grief-like behavior in the separation of a graylag goose from its mate: the first response to the disappearance of the goose's partner consists in the anxious attempt to find him again. The goose moves about restlessly by day and night, flying great distances and visiting places where the partner might be found, uttering all the time the penetrating trysyllable long-distance call. . . . The searching expeditions are extended farther and farther and quite often the searcher itself gets lost, or succumbs to an accident. . . . All the objective observable characteristics of the goose's behavior on losing its mate are roughly identical with human grief" (Lorenz, 1963, quoted in Parkes, 2001, as cited in Worden, 2008, p.15).

Are we searching for our lost person in this stage? Yes.

But it's more than just searching for the person. We are searching for the bond, the attachment. We are yearning for the emotions and connections we felt in that relationship. We are pining for the best part of ourselves that emerged in that relationship.

Phase 3: Despair and Disorganization

The third stage is Despair and Disorganization. If you're like me, this phase is a hellish place to reside.

Reading a work-related email that asked for my help on a fairly simple task, I'd cringe and feel like crawling under my desk. I'd want to reply, "You want me to look up a colleague's office number? My husband died! Don't you know I'm grieving? How can you ask me for hard things?"

June of 2018 was a tough month for my kids and me. Scott had been gone eight months. That June, my daughter and I went on a trip that Scott had planned for us before he'd died. My daughter graduated from high school (which had been a goal for him to live to see but didn't). Then there was our wedding anniversary, Father's Day, a friend's wedding, my birthday, and our daughter's graduation open house. Up next on the calendar: my brother's wedding (a brother who was also widowed by lung cancer).

Yes, looking back, June was an absolutely awful month for us.

I was overwhelmed, sad, and disorganized. I couldn't remember things. I was easily irritated. Indecisive. I barely got the invitations out for the graduation open house on time.

So, my two teens (who are clearly the children of a psychotherapist) took me aside while we were on a little hike one warm summer day.

We were standing near the base of a waterfall, feeling the spray on our faces in the late June sunshine, and my daughter said, "You look like you're doing okay. Now is the time for us to have an intervention."

Oh, great. I've never met a single person who was eager to be on the receiving end of an intervention.

She reached in her back pocked and pulled out a crumpled napkin from our earlier lunch at Dairy Queen to check the notes she'd written while I'd been in the restroom.

The boy stood behind her in solidarity. Taking a deep breath, she said: "We know these are tough firsts for you, and we know you are sad. We are sad too.

"When *we* are grieving, we need you to be there for us. We need you to hear us when we tell you we are struggling with other issues, too. You can't say, 'I can't help because I'm grieving' anymore. You have to say, 'I'm sorry you are struggling. How can I help?'"

Nope. Nobody wants to be the target of an intervention. This one was a doozy.

The lady who was presuming to know about grief; the grief counselor, for goodness sake, was being called out by her kids about she was handling her grief. (But aren't you impressed with their intervention? Oh, I'm just so proud.)

Looking back at that afternoon, my children were gently coaxing me out of this third phase by saying, "Enough with the despair, Mom. We need you to come back to us now."

Phase 4: Reorganization and Recovery (added by Parkes later)

Phase 4 is a time of reorganization and recovery. This is a positive adjustment in the grief process. The pain begins to retreat, and we start to see some hope. We might even explore new friendships and relationships.

We accept that our lives are forever changed, and while we still have moments of intense sadness, we are able to remember our relationship with our loved one with more joy and maybe with fewer tears. We find a new identity, new behaviors, new goals.

When my dad figured out how to use the oven and the microwave after my mom died, he discovered a passion for cooking he'd never imagined. I came home from college one weekend, and he'd made a pot roast with potatoes and carrots. It was actually tasty!

My mom had historically burned every dish she'd ever attempted to cook, but this meal my dad made was great. The meat was fall-apart tender and juicy, the vegetables were firm and delicious, and the sauce was flavorful.

My dad was discovering not only that food could taste good but also that he was the one who could create the flavors. This was a positive adjustment in the grief process. He discovered a new identity through new behaviors, which was right in the heart of this fourth phase.

I have found Bowlby and Parkes' theory of the Four Phases of Grief quite helpful. It gives insight into the stages one might navigate after a loved one dies.

However, this theory does not give us anything to *do* about our grief. These are phases that are passively observed rather than intentionally navigated.

The idea of severing bonds with the deceased is an issue of Bowlby's theory that I've struggled with. Parkes, going off of Bowlby's theory, later conducted some legitimate research on grief and he found that grief work/grief interventions are necessary.

Parkes believed grief work would include confronting the preoccupation with the deceased, working through the trauma of the loss experience, and making sense of the world without the loved one in it.

So, to sum up so far, Freud started the work; Kubler-Ross talked about stages of grief in the context of dying; Lindeman added insight by discussing tasks; Bowlby contributed to the theories through the lens of attachment; and Parkes added in his thoughts on the phases of grief.

But none of them held up a mirror to my own experiences with grief, until...

Continuing Bonds of Grief Theory

I had studied and researched grief, and I was disappointed with what I was finding. Nobody described what I was wrestling with. I was so frustrated with the advice to find closure. To walk away. To move on.

Then I read *Continuing Bonds* by Klass, Silverman, and Nickman (1996).

My friend, there is hope. There are reasonable theorists out there who said, "Hold the phone. We have a connection."

They begin with:

> *This book was conceived to give voice to an expanded view of the bereavement process. Specifically, this book re-examines the idea that the purpose of grief is to sever the bonds with the deceased in order to free the survivor to make new attachments. We offer an alternative model based on the mourner's continuing bonds with the deceased* (p. 3).

You read it right here, buddy.

The purpose of grief is *not* to disconnect from the person who died, but instead, to *reconnect*. We can continue the bond with the deceased. The purpose of grief is not to end the relationship, but to rebuild it.

This was a completely new paradigm in the '90s. In fact, if a person who was grieving attempted to maintain an attachment to the person who was dead, (s)he was diagnosed with a psychological problem like Unresolved Grief.

C'mon! Wanting to continue the relationship with the deceased is *not* a sign of lack of resolution. Wanting to stay in relationship is okay. It is, in fact, healthy.

The Continuing Bonds Theory holds that, not only is it okay to continue a bond with the deceased, it is advisable.

A widow or widower can talk to their dead spouse, laugh with them, even argue as they normally would. He can tell her she would LOVE the new political candidate and that, again, she would be wrong.

A widow can leave his side of the bed covered with his favorite blanket. A widower can place his late wife's favorite flowers on the table each spring.

Parents can devote a special part of themselves to parenting their dead child; continuing to celebrate birthdays, buying gifts on holidays to donate to a charity, or learning about something the child loved.

An adult daughter can walk down the aisle of her wedding and imagine her dad walking beside her. She can drape a tuxedo jacket on the back of the church pew where he would have been seated for the ceremony.

These are not pathological delusions or fantasies. These are basic requirements of grief work.

Oh, my friend, can I articulate clearly enough what a relief this is? After reading some of the terrible theories out there that had insisted that we find closure, that we end the relationship in order to move forward?

Some of the past practices of "re-griefing" even went so far as to force the grieving person to imagine the corpse as simply a decomposing figure in the ground and no longer the person they loved. These practices feel like cruel, torturous practices to the bereaved.

Granted, current culture hasn't necessarily caught on to this Continuing Bonds Model, so our friends and family are still telling us to "find closure" or to "let go."

Movies, music, novels, television shows tell us it's time to get over it and move on, which informs our friends and families that this is what is expected of us. This is a damaging message.

We don't need to find closure or move on.

Grief counselors and researchers should be up to speed on this Continuing Bonds Model. We need to encourage the practice of developing a continuing bond with the person who has died.

A widow can be encouraged to maintain a relationship with her husband, even if she remarries. The daughter can wear her dad's wedding ring on her thumb on her wedding day to feel him holding her hand. A parent is urged to buy gifts for the child who died and put the presents under the Christmas tree.

How long does the parent buy presents for the deceased child? Until she doesn't need to anymore.

Another facet provided by the Continuing Bonds Model is that we allow our grief to affect us for the rest of our life. We don't have to wrap it up within six months. Instead, we are changed by our grief, improved, made stronger and more resilient—transformed.

This is consistent with my experience of grief. I am tougher, smarter, more compassionate, and empathic, a kinder human being, a better friend, a sweeter sister, a more patient mother, and, perhaps someday, a more loving spouse *because* of my grief experience. As hard as this was, my bereavement has changed me for the better each time.

My grief has transformed me.

Worden's Tasks of Grief

Worden discusses the Continuing Bonds Process in his book, *Grief Counseling and Grief Therapy* (2008), which I think is one of the better books ever written on the topic of grief work.

While it is a book written to the mental health professional, I encourage laypersons to read it too. Despite holding academic appointments at both Harvard Medical School and Rosemead Graduate School of Psychology at the time of his most recent revision of the book, his writing is compassionate and readable.

While I won't summarize the whole book here (although it's tempting), I will talk about his theory of the goals and tasks of grief. Buckle in, friend. This is really good stuff.

First of all, Worden identifies four goals of grief:

1) Accept the reality of the loss;
2) Help the person deal with the emotional and behavioral distress;
3) Help the bereaved overcome obstacles to readjusting to the loss, and
4) Help one find a way to maintain a bond with the deceased while reinvesting in one's own life.

I know. Crazy good, right?

Okay, fine. Let me translate a little.

When we can tolerate the fact that the person is dead, we can self-soothe the hard emotions. When we can move forward into a new life and find a new place for the deceased, we have completed the goals of grief work.

But *how* do we do that?

Worden (2008) brilliantly assigns us four tasks to align with those goals. There's actual stuff we can *do* to propel us through this grief process toward resolution.

Worden admits most of us will do this on our own, in time, but that grief counselors can aid us if we get stuck or are suffering from one of the types of grief that are exacerbated by other issues.

Task I

The first task is to "**accept the reality of the loss**." This means to turn our face directly into the wind of this hard reality. We must confront the truth that the person is not coming back. They won't be joining us at the dinner table ever again. They won't be calling us on the phone. They won't need their clothes again. They are actually dead.

Joan Didion (2005) wrote a powerful story of her experience of longing for her husband's return in her book *The Year of Magical Thinking*. I'd read it during my first year of widowhood and kept saying, "Yep. Yes. Right. Precisely this."

Instead of accepting the reality of the loss, some of us sit in a place of denial, which can show up in various ways. Maybe we subtly believe they are away on a trip and will be coming back. We might hold on to their belongings in the hope they might need them again.

We might deny the meaning of the loss—we may demonize the person, saying he was a bad husband or she was difficult to live with. While it may be true, we focus on how they wronged us as a way of making the loss less significant than it really was.

Maybe we stay in a place of denial when we push away reminders of the person, refuse to look at photographs, remove all cues that might cause us to remember.

Others might deny the reality of the finality of the death by visiting a medium or other spiritualist in an attempt to communicate with their loved one.

Denial is a buffer from the harsh, unacceptable reality of the loss. We just can't face it.

Slowly, acceptance and denial dance together and war apart. There is a kind of concurrent knowing and not knowing the truth of the death.

How do we accomplish this task? Worden (2008) advises we *engage in rituals* that validate the reality of the death. We make it real by visiting the grave or the cremains, looking through photographs, remembering the person who is gone, and telling ourselves the truth about what and whom we've lost.

Worden (2008) also advises that we accomplish this task by *talking about the loss.* Find someone who cares about you, who will listen to your stories, who will simply be an ear while you process your losses.

Sadly, in our culture we are discouraged from talking about it; our friends might not know how to listen to us. Perhaps they are uncomfortable with awkward silences or deep emotion. The depth of loss is difficult for them to comprehend or the pain causes them discomfort which they don't know how to tolerate.

When my parents died, I needed to talk about them all the time. But I'd talk about them with people who weren't equipped to listen.

As a result, I felt shut down, unheard, unloved. It wasn't true. People did love me, and they weren't trying to shut me down or mute me. They just didn't know how to hear my story. So I had to find someone who did.

Grief counselors and grief support groups are a great place to begin to accomplish this task. Grief counselors, psychologists, and psychotherapists have skills and training to listen and provide comfort and insight. Grief support groups are structured specifically to encourage us to talk about our story as way of connecting to a shared narrative.

So, Task I of grief work, according to Worden (2008), is to accept the reality of the loss, and the way to do this is to engage in rituals and talk about the death.

Task II

The second task of Worden's is to "**work through the pain of grief**" (Worden, 2008).

He's not messing around, is he? He's pushing us right into the deep end of this grief work. Accept it. Feel it!

As I mentioned earlier and repeatedly, there are actual emotional, physical, behavioral, and cognitive symptoms of grief, and most of them hurt. We aren't just sad. We are angry, guilty, depressed, lonely. For most of us, the sheer pain and intensity of these feelings makes us to want to escape them.

Sometimes our friends and families don't help us. When we are in pain, they tell us we are being selfish or self-centered, that we've been carrying on long enough.

Six months after my husband died, my nurse told me I'd feel better if I started dating.

After nine months of grief, I was asked, "How long do you plan on grieving?"

The day after the first-year anniversary of Scott's death, a friend started a sentence with, "Now that the first year is up...."

I felt I was being placed on a deadline. They meant well. They just didn't want to see me in pain anymore.

But I couldn't rush it. I tried to explain, "I'm grieving as fast as I can!"

Sometimes people try to cheer us: "Be glad he's in a better place." "She wouldn't want you to be sad." "God just wanted another angel."

I know these people are trying their best to help us feel better. They are trying to distract us from our pain. But their attempts to soften our grief and lessen our pain end up hardening our grief and intensifying our pain because now we feel we aren't allowed to grieve in their presence.

Rather than suppressing our pain because it's intolerable to others, some of us suppress our pain because it feels intolerable to us.

Instead of confronting our distress, we engage in self-medication or self-destruction. Drinking alcohol numbs us. Other drugs soothe us. Retail therapy, compulsive overeating, gambling, sexual acting out, or other numbing behaviors become our friends.

As I mentioned earlier, however, this behavior compounds our problems because now we have the consequences of our unhealthy behaviors *and* we still have to deal with our grief.

No, the best thing we can do for ourselves in this grief, my beloved friend, is to learn how to sit with the pain.

Not many of us know how to sit with an unpleasant emotion. We feel something painful, and we run away as fast as we can. But grief is an insistent visitor. It's persistent. It will not be ignored forever.

Worden (2008) tells us it's wise to just experience it, even press in to it. (Please note: If you are struggling with a traumatic loss, you are experiencing ruminating thoughts, are having suicidal ideation, or are struggling with complex emotional reactions, I encourage you to seek help through a local mental health professional).

So, Task II is to work through the pain of grief, and to do that, we have to allow ourselves to actually feel the discomfort.

Task III

Worden's third task is to "**adjust to a world without the deceased**," and he identifies three areas where this needs to occur: external adjustment, internal adjustment, and spiritual adjustment.

External adjustment is subjective to the survivor and the relationship. It means adjusting to the new lifestyle without the person in it.

The secondary grief I mentioned earlier explores these kinds of losses: the death of a spouse might include the loss of a shopper, housekeeper, accountant, co-parent, lover, social calendar attendant, dance partner, companion, etc. After the spouse has died, there is a slow realization of all that they did as new challenges arise.

My car's transmission blew in the middle of a busy stoplight during rush hour last fall. (This is a great way to get an entire city to hate you.) Anyway, I immediately thought, "I need to call Scott."

Nope. Can't. He's dead.

It struck me that I needed him for a number of things in that moment: I needed transportation home. I needed a tow for the car. I would need an assessment on cost for repairs, and I needed to determine if the car was worth fixing (I knew it wasn't).

Then I needed to figure out what to do with the dead car.

I needed to buy a different car, which meant I needed to research car dealerships, do safety and value ratings, apply for a car loan, blah, blah, blah—all which had been Scott's domain when he was alive.

Those were all losses I hadn't really considered until I sat stalled in the middle of a busy intersection during afternoon rush hour traffic.

I'll admit I was angry that I had to deal with that. I am resentful that it's on me to remove the dead rodents from the patio after the cat hauls them up to the back door. I'm angry that I have to manage the bills and figure out how to live on half the income we had before he died.

I am indignant that I have to be both father and mother to two grieving adolescents who are high-need because of grief and age.

These are all external adjustments I've had to make because I am now a widow.

Ugh. A "widow." Terrible word. Terrible new identity. That identity is an internal adjustment.

The *internal adjustments* are so hard. We have to adjust to a new way of seeing and understanding ourselves. How does the death redefine us? Has it changed our self-efficacy? Has it impacted our self-esteem? Am I still "me" now that I'm not a part of an "us"?

This internal adjustment has been a bit of an existential crisis for me. I knew who I was before he was sick, before he died. I was competent. I was capable. I had impressive roles like, "Chair of the Department of Psychology" and "Director of the Humor Academy" and "President of the Board of Trustees of the Urban Cross-Cultural College Consortium."

I had titles, and I was good at those jobs. They gave me my identity.

But when we found out he was sick and was quickly dying, I stepped down from those roles.

I don't get to wake up to go do impressive jobs that I'm good at—not anymore. Instead, I am doing things that feel really hard for me and outside my skill-set (cooking, budgeting, vehicle maintenance, lawn care, snow removal), and my self-esteem is low. I don't feel competent or intelligent in the areas where I'm spending so much of my time and energy.

It's hard to grieve both the death of my husband and the loss of myself.

The internal challenges require us to explore our self-efficacy. If you had no control over that horrendous loss, do you have any control over anything? What *can* you still control?

We have to explore our self-image. Who are you now that he is no longer here? Who can you become?

I am emerging out of the fear and anxiety related to all these losses, and I am stepping into a new world where I am rediscovering me. It's an existential crisis, what Worden called a *spiritual adjustment.*

Spiritual adjustment is a time for identity redevelopment, deep in the core of ourselves. It's also a time of reckoning. Do we still believe what we used to believe about faith, about the world, and about God?

This is actually an exciting time, when we get there, of self-exploration and redefinition. Grief can be an opportunity for transformation.

We will explore this more in the final chapter.

Task IV

Worden's final task is to **"find an enduring connection with the deceased in the midst of embarking on a new life."**

This means we are to maintain a continuing bond with the person who has died but in a way that allows us to start a new life.

The opposite of this, according to Worden is "not living." If we close ourselves off to new relationships and new experiences, we are not living.

Worden admits this might be the most difficult task of the four, and that some of us get stuck here.

So how do we accomplish this? Well, the first half requires us to find a new way of relating to the person who has died.

This might seem impossible, but it's not. Think about it: how do you maintain other relationships in your life? I mean really. How do you maintain a friendship, for example?

You probably pay attention to the person. You dedicate energy to them. You care for that other person, honor their needs, and communicate with them.

The same can be done for your beloved person who died. Spend time thinking about her, do things in her honor, maybe write her letters or talk to her while you're washing dishes.

Create new rituals or honor old traditions. Find a way to transmit their values by extending them to others and keeping them with you. Do things you both enjoyed before. Find ways to remember them with humor.

The second half of this task is embarking on a new life. It means beginning again. Some of us don't really want to do this. We liked the old life. We want that old life back.

But those of us who stay in that old life aren't going to do very well because there is a significant part missing—the person who died. Trying to recapture what is left of that life will hurt us because as we continue to search for them in that old life we will be reminded that they are not coming back.

Embarking on a new life means getting out of bed. Brushing your teeth. Going to work. Just doing the next thing to get through the day.

Embarking on a new life means keeping the parts of the old life that work for you but now trying out new tasks. It means trying new hobbies, new jobs, new volunteer opportunities, and making new friends.

Embarking on a new life means being open to the hope that a new life might bring. Embarking on a new life is a commitment to making the deceased's life meaningful and their death redeemable.

If you think about the profound purpose embedded in this task, it is both terrific and terrifying. We will explore "purpose" in upcoming chapters.

The various theories, stages, and tasks of grief have given us a framework to consider the process of grief and the work that may need to be accomplished.

Keep in mind that many individuals navigate their grief very well without ever reading a book, attending a support group, going to therapy, or intentionally addressing the tasks of grief.

This information is valuable, however, to the person who wants to navigate their grief on purpose. For such a person, resilience is at the heart of purposeful grief.

In this next chapter, you will see where you are already profoundly resilient.

Finally! We get to talk about something *light*!

Melissa Mork

Resilience

When my husband died, three friends sent me copies of *Option B: Facing Adversity, Building Resilience, and Finding Joy* by Sheryl Sandberg and Adam Grant. It was such a cheerful, polished, optimistic view of the grief experience. I found it well-written, insightful, and encouraging. While much of it resonated, there were parts that also gave me pause.

Sandberg's husband died suddenly and unexpectedly, and she was left to parent her two children alone. My husband died quickly after a very short, four and a half month fight with an aggressive cancer, and I was left to parent my two children alone.

But when she was giving commencement addresses at Ivy League schools in the first year of her grief, I was still hiding in my house, with embarrassingly low personal hygiene, wondering if the kids would notice I was wearing the same sweatshirt four days in a row ("Mom, is that mac 'n cheese stain on your shirt from *Monday*?").

She seemed to have bounced back so quickly from her grief, ready to move on and continue to conquer life and the world. I came out of a walking-talking-grief-coma at the end of year one and stepped in to year two wondering why it actually felt *harder*.

I think I sometimes bristled at Sandberg and Grant's *Option B* book because it felt like this was a race and maybe I was losing.

I wanted to expedite my grief. Trust me, I was grieving as fast as I could. At one point in the first year, I was attending three different grief support groups, plus individual therapy. A friend even asked me, "Do you think you might be overdoing this grief *work* thing?"

No matter what I tried, though, I couldn't accelerate the process. In the end, I had to just follow the course of my grief in its own time. I had to process my loss at my own speed.

Did my slow, snail-like pace mean I wasn't resilient? Nope. I was resilient, and so are you.

Resilience doesn't mean conquering something. Resilience in grief doesn't mean triumph over sadness. Being resilient doesn't mean feeling completely joyful all the time. Resilience in grief has nothing to do with finding closure, moving on, or getting over it.

In fact, even though we are resilient, we will shut down at times. We will feel completely, devastatingly overwhelmed. We'll be ambushed by memories, ambuscaded by hard feelings, we'll still weep on the anniversaries. We will feel chronic sadness over our loss, maybe for a lifetime.

Resilience in grief means we survive it. Resilience in grief demands that we take the time we need.

Think about the deepest kinds of physical wound: a gun shot, a stab wound, an open-heart surgery, or an amputation. Does this kind of injury heal quickly? Just think: the deepest physical wound heals more quickly than the severing of human relationship.

In my faith, there is the belief that, when two people marry, they become one flesh (Genesis 2:24). They merge their lives and fuse together. It's a beautiful concept.

So when one of us dies, there is a tearing apart of that one flesh. One is physically severed from the other. The survivor has to heal from that emotional, psychological, social, and spiritual amputation. How quickly does that heal?

If you've borne a child from your own body, or grown him or her in your heart through adoption, and that child dies, that part of your heart feels ripped out of you. How fast does that wound heal?

If you've loved a parent for your whole life, with the first breath that expanded your chest, and then that parent dies and leaves you behind to breathe alone, how quickly can that heal?

Must we be in such a rush?

When we have a physical wound, even a minor laceration, the first thing we do is triage the injury. We apply pressure and raise the injured part above heart level to slow the flow of blood. We lightly clean the area with soft towels and gentle soaps or solutions. We look for debris in the wound to make sure there isn't anything left that might interfere with healing. We might apply a salve or ointment to prevent infection, and we cover the injury with bandages to keep it protected from drying out or getting dirty.

Every day, until the wound is close to healing fully, we inspect it: changing the bandage when it's wet or dirty, looking for signs of infection, checking to see if there are any changes in the appearance of the injury.

Blood rushes to the location and brings oxygen and nutrients to grow new blood vessels and capillaries. White blood cells make chemical messengers that instruct the cells to create collagen and rebuild tissue.

What parallels can we bring to caring for the psych-ache of grief, the wound of having our loved one ripped from us?

In grief work, the first thing we have to do is triage. We put all of our focus on the loss, and we elevate the grief above almost everything else. My focus for the first few months after Scott died was almost exclusively on my sadness, my numbness, and tending to my children.

The physical injury requires delicate treatment of the areas around the wound. In grief, we treat the bereaved with gentleness.

People brought over food and sent gift cards. Friends hired a snow removal service for the first winter so I wouldn't have to shovel snow in the hard Minnesota winter.

When the kids and I were hard hit with the flu two months after Scott died, I made brief mention of it on Facebook and then went and took a nap. When I woke up and wandered into the kitchen, my table was piled high with cans of chicken noodle soup, loads of paper towels, Clorox Clean-up wipes, Lysol spray, luxury toilet paper, and a case of 7-up. Friends treated us very tenderly.

Like a physical wound, we need to look for debris that might impede the healing process. For me, I was experiencing some symptoms of severe trauma which were complicating my grief work. I sought out professional assistance—I saw a therapist who specialized in trauma to help me clean out some of that emotional debris that was interfering with my healing.

Similar to how we might apply salves and bandage our wounds, in our grief, we might seek out other kinds of comfort and protection. Some read scripture or poetry or motivational literature. Others seek out comfort from friends and loved ones. We might look at photographs, reminisce about our loved one, or go places where we might feel closer to the person who's gone.

With a physical injury, we inspect the site. Is it healing okay? Is there infection?

In our grief, we inspect our process. Am I doing this right? Is this normal? Is there something that is making my grief harder?

In our grief process, like our bodies with a physical wound, our hearts begin to mend, particularly when the grief environment is protected and nourished. With time and care, we recover. It is built into all of us, this healing process. Physically, our bodies take over and heal. Emotionally, in grief, we do the same. We are resilient. We bounce back.

It is important for me to point out that resilient people are not resilient because their lives are easier than the rest of us. Resilient people cope effectively in difficult times. Some of us are resilient *because* we have encountered adversity, hardship, and even devastating personal losses.

In the following sections, I will talk about factors in resilience that allow us to heal.

Resilience

Resilience is the human ability to recover from stress, adversity, even trauma. It means being adaptable in stressful situations. Resilience is the tension between accepting that adversity is going to happen to us, and trusting that we will not break.

Think of the most resilient thing in your house right now. It's probably in your junk drawer or your office desk; maybe it's in your kid's mouth if she has orthodontia; or it's wrapped around the stems of some broccoli in your fridge. You know what I'm talking about: the rubber band.

The rubber band is stretchy, malleable, bendy, but it always snaps back to its original shape, regardless of the amount of (reasonable) tension we apply to it. The rubber band is the model of resilience.

Now, applying this analogy further, yes, the rubber band can break when there is too much stress applied: when the stress is unremitting and lasts for years. When the rubber has been exposed to sunlight, the polymers and plasticizers deteriorate, and it loses its flexibility.

Exposure to ultraviolet light causes the polymer and plasticizer chains to break, and the rubber band becomes dry, causing it to crack and crumble. When it's cold, the rubber band becomes brittle and prone to snapping.

But when protected, cared for (like applying natural oil to it, for example) rubber bands can last a very long time and maintain their resilience.

I know. You just paused on that and wondered, "Does this lady *oil* her rubber bands?"

No, I'm not *that* lady. You can get a ball of rubber bands for $3 at Target. You get them with your produce or wrapped around your mail, for goodness' sake.

No, I don't sit and oil my rubber bands. Usually I pull them back on my pointer finger and aim them at my kid and yell, "INCOMING!" and then the rubber bands hit the wall and disappear behind the couch.

My point of mentioning the application of natural oil is that oil can nourish and maintain resilience in something as commonplace as a rubber band. We are much more precious than rubber bands, so our own nourishing self-care can take us a very long way in protecting our resilience.

We are all born with some degree of resilience. Some have more, some have less. When we look at survivors of human atrocities, natural disasters, childhood trauma, most of them have shown tremendous, jaw-dropping resilience. It isn't something we either have or we don't. We are all born with some level of resilience.

There are things we can do to build and maintain our psych-emotional flexibility.

Please take note, though, that resilience does *not* mean we don't feel pain. It doesn't mean we don't experience the stresses, the fear, the anger, or the other emotions associated with grief. Resilient people suffer. We all suffer.

Resilient people aren't destroyed by suffering. We don't snap under pressure. We don't break when we face adversity.

Bonanno (2004) finds that many people will endure major life losses, including the death of a loved one, with very little interruption in their functioning. Their grief is quiet and non-disruptive. They are able to tolerate their grief and live with it as they continue to work, parent, go to church, and live their lives. Most people demonstrate profound resilience when confronted with loss.

The Penn Resilience Program led by Dr. Martin Seligman is part of the premiere research program on positive psychology at the University of Pennsylvania. Resilience is one of the factors of positive psychology they continually research and teach.

In their research, they have identified six core skills that we can learn and develop to build resilience: self-awareness, self-regulation, mental agility, strength of character, connection, and optimism. In the following sections, I will address each of these with some descriptions and stories that can help us make sense of them.

Self-Awareness

According to the Penn Resilience Program, self-awareness is the "ability to pay attention to your thoughts, emotions, behaviors, and physiological reactions" to events. This is the beginning of resilience.

When I reflect on the emotional experiences of grief, it is almost overwhelming to even describe, let alone live with. If you've grieved, you already know.

You feel shock. Numbness. Disorganized thoughts. Nothing makes sense, and you're lost.

There is a heaviness deep in your core. Your heart literally aches. You wonder if it might be broken. If you could maybe die from the actual pain.

You feel so sad it squeezes you like a vice. The sorrow crashes over you like waves. You are buffeted; clinging to a tiny life raft in a raging storm at sea.

You're angry. Livid. Enraged.

Sometimes you're just really annoyed and bitter.

But you're also terrified. You have butterflies in your stomach. Panic tightens in your chest.

And guilt. You have so much guilt and regret. It can be crippling, the guilt.

These aren't light or easy emotions, my friend. These are big. So when I talk about self-awareness, I am taking you to a place of significant reflection on your emotional intelligence.

I would describe Emotional Intelligence (EQ) as your ability to recognize and accurately label your emotions, to express your emotions in healthy ways, and to use your emotions appropriately, especially to move you to resolution or move you toward your goals.

Another layer of emotional intelligence is the ability to recognize and facilitate the expression of emotions in others, but that's not my focus here. There are many other definitions of EQ but the underlying theme is the ability to know and use your emotions instead of letting your emotions control you.

How can this possibly happen with the intensity of emotions I listed earlier? Those weren't light emotions like disappointment or concern. These are sharp, jagged boulders of emotion.

When Scott had been gone about fifteen months, I lost two significant friendships within five days of each other. Both had been major sources of support and companionship for me in my previous year of intense grief.

But one of the friendships had grown irreparably unhealthy, and I felt compelled to end it, while the other loss was not on my terms. After the second friendship failed due to catastrophic miscommunication, I was stunned and overwhelmed: already grieving my husband's death, and then reeling from the loss of my two closest friends.

As I sat in a chair, staring into the middle distance of my living room, holding a cup of coffee as it grew cold in my hands, I had to recognize my feelings, and I had to label them: I was sad. Desperately *sad*.

I was also really *afraid* of losing the support. I was *angry* that I was being left. I felt *lonely* because the people I would have called to talk this through were the people I was grieving (including my husband).

Self-awareness is key in emotional intelligence because if the goal is to manage and use your emotions, you first have to know what they are.

How do we develop this habit of self-awareness? You start by checking in with yourself and asking, "What am I feeling right now?"

For me, I have to pay attention to my physical experiences. When you notice an emotion is rising, what's happening in your chest? Is there tension in your neck? Are you clenching your teeth? My grief usually feels like a burning hot pressure in my sternum.

Then we have to accurately label the emotion. But be careful *how* you label them. Sometimes the context is going to tell you one thing, but the truth behind the emotion might be something else.

Let me explain.

Back in 1962, Schachter and Singer conducted a study at the University of Minnesota where they injected male research participants with epinephrine (adrenaline) that caused increased heart rate, rapid breathing, trembling, and other excitatory responses. The young men were each told the shot was a vitamin that could affect visual skills. The misleading information was given to prohibit skewing the results.

With adrenaline pumping through their bodies, each participant was then placed in a room with a person who was "in" on the study and acted in one of two ways: euphoric or angry.

The researchers found that the participants who were saturated with happiness in the "euphoric" room would label their current emotion as happy, while the participants who were blanketed with rage in the "angry" room would interpret their current feeling as anger.

Isn't this interesting? The physical experiences were exactly the same because of the shots of adrenaline. But each participant had taken on the emotion of those they were near, simply by applying the label that was most available to him.

I find I do this sometimes. When I have an emotional reaction to something, I will explain it away by the current context. I use the emotion word most readily available to me. It'd be more accurate if I paused and reflected on what I'm *really* feeling.

Here's an example: before I speak to a large audience, I get serious butterflies. My breathing gets shallow. My hands are sweaty. I have to pee. As I stand backstage, ready to be introduced, my heart pounds so hard I can hear it in my head. I get a little light-headed, and my mind goes blank.

Am I in love? Am I grief-stricken? Am I angry? Am I overjoyed? Am I terrified? Yep! My physical experience could mean any one of those things.

If I really think about it, though, I can label the emotion accurately: I'm going to be standing in front of a group of people who are eager to hear what I have to say, and I think I'm going to have some fun out there. I'm going to connect with the audience, see their smiles, hear their laughs, and maybe even make them cry.

Based on the context, the accurate emotion I'm feeling is excitement.

What happens if I label my emotions inaccurately? What if I tell myself I'm terrified? I'll choke on my words. I'll sweat profusely. I'll hyperventilate. I won't do very well in my presentation because I just lied to myself about what I'm feeling, and my brain and body will believe the lie.

What if I'm exhausted when I get home from work, and I'm getting irritated by simple inconveniences? If I've labeled my emotion as anger, I will have to scan my house for what I can be mad at. I'll pick a fight with my daughter, or I might yell at my son for something inconsequential.

If I accurately label it as fatigue, being overwhelmed, and feeling pressured that I still have to cook dinner, tidy the house, and do some final grading, I'm more accurate. I can take a breath and step back, dealing with the emotion that *is* rather than the emotion that *isn't*.

I can address the problem that is triggering the emotion by taking a break. I can ask my kids to tidy up. I can call a friend to talk through work stress. We can eat popcorn and apples for dinner. Again.

Self-Regulation

The Penn Resilience Project identifies the next resilience factor as self-regulation. This is the "ability to alter how we think, feel, behave, and respond to a situation toward a desired goal."

What this means is that we must learn to move beyond labeling our emotions to *managing* our emotions. We can do this by getting some perspective.

Yes, your grief is heavy and intense. But can that intensity last forever? No. I promise that it cannot.

Will the heaviness of this grief *actually* crush you? While it feels like it might, I promise it will not.

Because you're grieving, you're too sad to go out with friends tonight. In the scope of eternal life, does cancelling those plans matter? I promise you it does not.

How we *think* about a situation or a stressor is going to affect the emotions we feel. If you think to yourself, "This is never going to get better," you will feel defeated.

Are there truths buried in that statement of "This is never going to get better"? No. I have to rewrite the wording to be more accurate. "This will never get better" is more honestly stated as "This will someday get better."

Of course, this is the hardest thing you have ever done, and of course you're feeling discouraged. But you're also reading this and working toward healing, so it *will* someday feel better.

The second part of the definition of self-regulation is altering how we *feel* about a situation.

How am I supposed to change the way I feel in my grief? Is it even possible to change our emotions?

Yes, it is. We have a choice every day, every moment, to select our emotions. It requires awareness of what we are feeling (self-awareness from the last section) and accurate labeling.

Then it requires a change in perspective.

I'm not a fan of clichés, and I've heard some doozies in my grief journeys. One of them is, "Be glad you had him in your life for as long as you did."

Please don't tell me to be glad about anything regarding my husband's death.

But, there is a nugget of truth in that platitude: I *am* in need of some gratitude. I can look at our 28-year marriage and remember the joy in it. There is *so* much for which I am grateful.

I can shift my emotions from heavy to light by closing my eyes and recalling a happier memory. I can shift my feelings by changing my focus.

The final part of self-regulation is to alter our *behaviors* and *responses.*

I have a dear friend whom I love deeply. We had arranged to get together one evening, but he had forgotten we'd made plans and he scheduled something else for the same night. When he realized the error, he didn't cancel the new plans. Instead he bailed on me.

I was really hurt. My emotional margins were already compromised by grief, recent broken friendships, hard parenting, heavy workload, and exhaustion. There were no excuses for it, but I lashed out. I tend not to get angry easily ("Really?" you ask. "Didn't you yell at a Home Health Aide and throw her out of your house?"), but that evening, I was really upset.

In lashing out, I hurt my friend with my words. I did not self-regulate.

Looking back, my regret is that I *reacted* to my hurt rather than *responded* to the source of the problem. Reacting is knee-jerk, automatic, habitual, and often thoughtless. Responding is mindful, intentional, and purposeful.

Had I taken a moment to reflect on what I was feeling, if I had labeled it, then articulated it and asked for help in finding a solution, the friendship would not have taken such a hit.

Existential psychologists believe that we are responsible and response-able, meaning we have an obligation to respond to events and other people with intention and purpose because we are able.

This concept of self-regulation supports this. Resilient people are response-able because they self-regulate their behaviors and responses.

The important piece in this section on self-regulation is that we manage our emotions and become aware of the goals we want to set for our grief work. In the next chapter on coping, we will discuss more tangible and practical ways to self-regulate and to set goals.

Mental Agility

Resilience researchers recognize the importance of mental agility, as well. This is a fancy phrase for being flexible in how we see and solve problems. Maybe you've seen brain games advertised online or offered in your phone's app store. Maybe you've heard that puzzles like crosswords and Sudoku are good for your brain.

It's true. Research on brain health has shown that problem solving and brain training games can exercise the areas of brain function that improve memory and enhance other cognitive function including resilience and problem solving.

But mental agility also refers to the ability to roll with the punches of life, so to speak. We are resilient when we are able to bend and not break.

Being agile is being able to experience the stresses of life— even the big ones like grieving the death of a loved one— without feeling completely broken, overwhelmed, or powerless. Agility means feeling capable to handle the hard things even though they are wholly unpleasant.

Another word that has emerged in current research related to resilience is "grit." (I know, it reminds me of the John Wayne movie, too).

Grit is passion and perseverance. It's the relentless pursuit of a goal. It's the characteristic within you that frames setbacks and hardships as challenges worth conquering rather than reasons to be discouraged.

Grit seems to matter in school, for example. Students with grit tend to have higher achievement in school, higher long-term academic success. In the workplace, grit is the focused pursuit of a completed project.

But in grief, grit might mean doggedly pursuing the tasks of grief (see Worden, chapter 2). Grit might mean finding a support group in order to talk about your loss (Task 1), or you might see grit in your determination to feel every one of those emotions, no matter how distressing they may be (Task 2).

Perhaps your grit is in the determined decision to find a new way to love the person who has died, and to spend time each day focused on that relationship with him or her (Worden's Task 4).

Another important factor of mental or cognitive agility is problem-solving ability. We are resilient when we can come face-to-face with a challenge and can creatively find a solution.

It may seem that some of us were born with stronger skills in problem solving while some of us get overwhelmed with organizing the forks in the silverware drawer. The good news is that we can all improve our problem-solving abilities.

What are some ways to enhance our problem-solving skills?

Let's start with self-care. We are more adept at solving problems (from simple puzzles all the way up to how to remodel our kitchens or how to solve a budget crisis at the church) when we are well nourished, refreshed, and well rested.

Have you ever been so tired and hungry that you are just unbearable to be around? Someone asks you what you want for dinner, and you can't even think straight?

On past family vacations, the four of us would go and go and go, and then, when we were all exhausted and overly hungry, we would finally stop the activities and discuss food options. This was never a good idea. Scott, in particular, would get "hangry" and impatient and indecisive, extending the delay of actually getting food in his belly.

On our last family vacation before Scott died, our twelve-year-old son asked me if he could buy a big bag of almonds at the airport while we were waiting to board the plane. Of course, I agreed, but I was puzzled by his request because nuts weren't usually his snack of choice.

I realized his stealth genius later that night. We'd checked in to the hotel but the dinner hour had passed and we hadn't eaten. We were all tired and hungry, and Scott started getting impatient when discussing what we should eat.

The kid quietly pulled out his bag of almonds from his backpack and handed them to Scott, who took a handful, passed the bag around, and we all had a calm conversation about what we wanted to eat for a late dinner while we crunched on almonds.

Our boy showed us a great problem-solving strategy. When hungry, eat something. Novel!

Basic self-care is sometimes rare, but it is imperative. Keeping ourselves nourished, exercised, well-rested and healthy will create resilience by enhancing our ability to tolerate emotions and to solve problems well.

The last piece of mental agility I'd like to encourage is the use of humor to shift your perspective. Samson, Glassco, Lee & Gross (2014) explored the effects of humorous coping on emotional regulation.

To evaluate this, researchers showed participants a series of difficult pictures—men with weapons, dog having surgery, a man with sutures in his forehead—and then neutral pictures— a fork, a chess board, an apple.

Some participants were then asked to provide humorous evaluations while others were asked for serious ones. An example of a humorous response to the man with sutures in his forehead, "He's got a great start to a zombie costume," while a serious one would be, "Good that he was able to seek medical attention." After a week, the participants were asked to rate the photos again.

Based on the results, researchers concluded that, while participants found it more difficult to find a humorous response to difficult photos, when they were successful, these interpretations were useful in enhancing positive emotions and reducing negative emotions in the moment. It was also helpful in down-regulating or reducing negative emotions in the long term.

How does this help us in grief? Shifting our perspective in a difficult moment can be challenging, but it can also provide levity, lift our mood, and help us locate our joy. Using humor can help us reduce the harder emotions in the long run.

When Scott was hospitalized for an extended time, he developed delirium. He called me (apparently delirium didn't halt his ability to use his cell phone) and gravely informed me that he was now a CIA operative and there was an entire army of tiny men in black ops uniforms hiding under his bed.

It was immediately clear to me that he was delusional. I raced over and met my sister-in-law in Scott's hospital room to make sure Scott was okay. I was panicked and upset.

But then my sister-in-law looked at me and said, "He's so cute like this."

Cute? This was an option? I could think of this as cute?

Well, yes, I could. He was safe. He was contained. He was on medication to address the delirium and restore him relatively quickly.

In the meantime, I was very safe because I was sitting next to James Bond, 007, and protected by tiny men dressed as black operatives who were hiding under his bed.

The value of looking for humor in a hard situation is this: when you are in the middle of the problem, it's all you can see. It becomes a blindfold. It occludes everything else. You can't see context. You can't see solutions. You only see the problem.

But what if you try to think of a funny way to see it? Your attempt to see it from a different direction is going to shift your perspective.

Suddenly the problem no longer blocks your entire view. You have peripheral vision. You can see context; you can see background; maybe even solutions.

You still have the blindfold, but with a sense of humor it becomes a simple piece of fabric that you can now tie into a cowboy mask or a jaunty neck scarf.

Character Strengths
Peterson and Seligman (2004) identified six core virtues valued by theologians and philosophers that contain certain character strengths.

The six virtues and their character strengths are as follows. Where do you see yourself in these?

Values in Action (VIA) classification of six virtues and 24 strengths of character. (Peterson and Seligman, 2004)

Virtue I. Wisdom and knowledge: cognitive strengths that entail the acquisition and use of knowledge.
(1) Creativity: thinking of novel and productive ways to do things
(2) Curiosity: taking an interest in all of ongoing experience
(3) Open-mindedness: thinking things through and examining them from all sides
(4) Love of learning: mastering new skills, topics, and bodies of knowledge
(5) Perspective: being able to provide wise counsel to others

Virtue II. Courage: emotional strengths that involve the exercise of will to accomplish goals in the face of opposition, external or internal.
(6) **Bravery: not shrinking from threat, challenge, difficulty, or pain**
(7) Persistence: finishing what one starts
(8) Honesty/Authenticity: speaking the truth and presenting oneself in a genuine way
(9) **Zest: approaching life with excitement and energy**

Virtue III. Humanity: interpersonal strengths that involve 'tending and befriending' others.

(10) Love: valuing close relations with others

(11) Kindness: doing favors and good deeds for others

(12) Social intelligence: being aware of the motives and feelings of self and others

Virtue IV. Justice: civic strengths that underlie healthy community life.

(13) Teamwork: working well as member of a group or team

(14) Fairness: treating all people the same according to notions of fairness and justice

(15) Leadership: organizing group activities and seeing that they happen

Virtue V. Temperance: strengths that protect against excess.

(16) Forgiveness: forgiving those who have done wrong

(17) Modesty: letting one's accomplishments speak for themselves

(18) Prudence: being careful about one's choices; not saying or doing things that might later be regretted

(19) Self-regulation: regulating what one feels and does

Virtue VI. Transcendence: strengths that forge connections to the larger universe and provide meaning.

(20) Appreciation of beauty and excellence: noticing and appreciating beauty, excellence, and/or skilled performance in all domains of life

(21) Gratitude: being aware of and thankful for the good things that happen

(22) **<u>Hope: expecting the best and working to achieve it</u>**

(23) Humor: liking to laugh and joke; bringing smiles to other people

(24) Religiousness/Spirituality: having coherent beliefs about the higher purpose and meaning of life

Martinez-Marti and Ruch (2017) found that "character strengths" predict resilience better than any of the other factors of resilience. In an examination of these character strengths, the three individual strengths that seemed to show the strongest relationships with resilience were zest, bravery, and hope (Martinez-Marti and Ruch, 2017).

Even as I write those three words, I feel my shoulders rising, my chin lifting, my chest expanding.

Zest!

Bravery!

Hope!

Keep in mind these three strengths are already inside each of us, fueling our resilience. We don't have to create or manufacture them. We've already got them.

In terms of our grief, these three factors can have profound impact on our resilience as we navigate through this process.

Zest is "approaching life with excitement and energy." Bravery means we aren't "shrinking from threat, challenge, difficulty, or pain." Both of these are in the virtue of "Courage" which is "emotional strengths that involve the exercise of will to accomplish goals in the face of opposition, external or internal." And hope? Hope is defined as "expecting the best and working to achieve it" (Martinez-Marti and Ruch, 2107, p.111).

Zest. What a great word. Zest is appetite, relish, an enthusiasm for life. It is reveling in the simple pleasures as much as the complex ones.

My mother didn't eat dessert. After dinner, while the rest of us would be eating our ice cream, she'd be finishing up the rest of the green beans. She just didn't care for sweet foods.

But she loved the sweetness of overripe fruit. She would stand, leaning over the sink, and she'd bite into a slightly brown, overly soft pear, and let the juice just run down her chin. She loved plums that would burst when she bit in to them. The juicier the fruit, the more she relished it.

My mother lived her life the way she ate fruit: with zest, with relish. She painted. She wrote poetry and prose. She ran. She danced. She laughed loud and lived expansively.

I'd like to think I've embraced her zest for life. In the last few years, I've learned to throw pots on the pottery wheel and run the kiln to finish them. I've learned to use a TIG welder. I've taken a glass-blowing class. I am now PADI certified in scuba diving. I'm taking new risks and learning new hobbies. I wake up wondering who I will get to meet today and what I might get to learn.

How can zest impact resilience in grief?

Scott knew (and loved) my zest for life. He would laugh and shake his head when I'd get a new idea. My yearning and sadness over the death of my husband remains, but I know that my life on earth has to continue even though his didn't.

My zeal for this life doesn't diminish my sadness. It does, however, make the sadness bearable as I snowshoe through the quiet, hushed woods or paddle-board the lake by my campus.

My desire to learn new things and meet new people can give me something to write about when I write letters to Scott at night, imagining him chuckle and shake his head reading them.

Your zest for life can counterbalance your experience of loss. Living this life in spite of the loss can transform into living this life because it is a gift.

Bravery. What is braver than stepping in to a new life without the person you've loved? What is more courageous than living with empty arms, in an empty house, sleeping in an empty bed?

Scott would often tell our kids that bravery isn't living without fear. It's stepping into the face of fear. It's doing something that scares the living daylights out of you. It's leaning in to the distress instead of hiding away from it. He'd tell them that being brave means getting back on that horse after he throws you.

I watched my children, ages thirteen and seventeen, walk down the middle aisle of the church toward their father's casket that morning of the funeral. They were terrified of all that this would entail, and they walked toward it anyway. I was astounded by their bold act of bravery.

And you—as you get out of bed in the morning after a night of tossing and turning and choose to make coffee and brush your teeth and go to work, even as your heart is aching for your child—you are the most courageous person in this world.

You, my friend, may feel anxious, shaking, terrified, but your daring act of stepping into a new day is pure guts and valor.

This is what makes you resilient.

Hope. As a person of faith, I have great hope. I believe that I will see my husband again. And I continue to maintain and nourish my faith with that hope in mind.

Resilient people maintain hope that they will have a strong future. Resilient people hope tomorrow is as bright (or brighter) than today. They have confidence that what they are doing today is going to have a positive impact on tomorrow. Resilient people anticipate things will work out in their favor, and they put effort into achieving that outcome.

Grieving is a profound act of hope. We grieve because we seek to be whole again. We demonstrate hope when we decide to keep on living. We manifest hope when we choose to do the hard work of grief.

But hope is an amazing shape shifter. It shows up differently depending on where we are in our grief process.

I had hope that Scott's treatment would give him years to live. The treatment failed, and the cancer grew.

I hoped he still had months and could live to see the kids start the new school year. He only had weeks and missed out on the end of their summer.

Then I had hope that his last few days would be sweet and peaceful, but instead they were painful and traumatic.

Still, I didn't lose hope. My hope shifted to him having a beautiful death.

He did.

After he died, I found new hope. I hope that my children will still find moments of happiness. I hope that my husband will remain in our lives somehow. I have hope that we will move forward with joy.

I hope my grief has a purpose. I hope that my grief experience will help you. I hope this is all for the Glory of God.

I hope. I hope. I hope.

Resilient hope is incandescent and diffuse. It doesn't shine on one single outcome. We hope for one thing, and when it does not come, we hope anew. When pain is most intense, the flame of hope may dwindle to a mere flicker, but still it patiently waits. As the despair begins to lift, hope flares into that dark space and blazes again.

Maybe that's the one thing to hope for in our loss: a flicker of light even in the darkest part of the mourning.

Connection

We have discussed the importance of self-awareness, self-regulation, mental agility, and character strengths as factors of resilience. Researchers in the Penn Resilience Program also agree that connection is significant to our resilience.

How important is connection and social interaction? We are designed to be in relationship. In fact, it can be a matter of life and death.

In infants, "failure to thrive" is now used as an umbrella term to cover a variety of concerns around slowed growth. But the term was first coined when observing babies who were dying of unknown reasons in the early 20th century.

In some orphanages and foundling hospitals in the US and the UK in the early 1900s, death rates of infants were close to 100%. Close to 100%! This was an unexplained human crisis.

The babies were being fed, changed, and kept safe in their cribs. Staff were instructed to wear surgical masks when they were near the infants. Nurses were to limit their interactions with the children. Staff worked hard to meet the babies' basic physical needs. Visitors could not visit freely with the infants for fear of spreading infections to the babies. Concerns for infant health were high, but the babies were still dying.

What were they dying from?

While their basic physical needs were being met very well, they were not provided human contact.

They were starved for physical touch, affection, love, connection.

We are wired for contact and human connection. The absence of contact is painful to us. Even deadly. Social isolation is used as punishment: prisoners of war, criminals, even recalcitrant students are punished with social separation.

If isolation and lack of connection can be used as the ultimate punishment, then human connection must be a fundamental human need.

In terms of resilience and grief, this is a significant piece of information. The death of a loved one, especially one who was our primary source of contact and connection, is extremely painful. That person was as critically important to our life as food and drink and shelter.

Our need for human connection continues after they've gone. Worden (2008) tells us in his fourth task that we must relocate the deceased in order to foster an enduring connection with them after they've died. We need to nurture that continuing bond.

We must locate other sources of connection, as well. Talking with a loved one is a start. Receiving a long hug from a friend can meet that contact need. Eye contact with a stranger can even help you to feel connected (you can web search the "4-Minute Experiment" with Amnesty International for a moving demonstration of this).

Chatting with a friend, sitting with others in a religious service, laughing with coworkers, volunteering to help another person or group: all of these can help us feel connected.

And, if I'm going to talk about grief and human connection, let me underscore that it is critically important to connect with others around your grief.

It might be especially helpful to talk with others who are also grieving the death of your loved one; the ones who loved him best also need to talk about him, so reach out and remember him together. Access your personal relationships to stay connected.

Optimism

Winston Churchill once said, "A pessimist sees the difficulty in every opportunity; an optimist sees the opportunity in every difficulty."

The well-known philosopher, Anonymous, says, "Optimism is the cheerful frame of mind that enables the teakettle to sing though in hot water up to its nose."

Are you an optimist? If you are, be very proud. This is a significant factor in resilience.

If you are a person of faith, current research shows that religion and faith play a key role in optimism. People of faith believe that life is meaningful, that they are part of something larger.

Attending regular religious services enhances optimism and resilience. This may be due to the content of the messages delivered in the services, or it may be related to the social interactions we have when we regularly attend and build friendships there.

The Christian optimist believes that "All things work together for good to those who love God, to those who are called according to His purpose" (Romans 8:28).

Purpose is a big part of this concept of optimism. Optimism isn't the same as naïve or mindless happiness. Optimism is confidence in a successful future. Optimism is directed, intentional, dedicated hope.

What does optimism in resilience have to do with grief?

If we revisit the tasks of mourning according to Worden (2008), I see grief as incredibly optimistic. While we work toward accepting the reality of the loss, experiencing the pain of it, and adjusting to a world without the person in it, the fourth task calls on us to continue a relationship with the person who has died, but to also step out into a new life.

What an optimistic charge: to relocate the person to a new place in your life and in your heart while you embark on a new journey. This holds intoxicating hope and purpose.

This means I can carry Scott in my heart, and he and I can explore new paths of this life with confidence that I'm going to be okay. I can be optimistic that I will be strong and successful in this new life, and that I don't have to abandon him in the process.

I am highly optimistic.

In the next section I will discuss coping strategies in grief. Coping strategies are ways to take these factors of resilience and apply them in tangible ways. Therefore, I will have many more practical techniques to help us develop resilience and navigate through our grief in the next section. Stay with me.

Coping and Creating Change

My son was twelve years old when his dad was diagnosed. At twelve, a boy is on the precipice of so many developmental leaps: puberty, adolescence, peer pressure, romantic crushes, middle school, then high school, extracurriculars, his first job.

He will learn to shave, to drive, to be a man. All without his dad.

Imagine the internal challenges for this boy. At the time around Scott's death, "toxic masculinity" was a term being used in cultural conversations. What were the rules of manhood? Did he have to be silent and stoic? Could he even express emotion?

Shortly after Scott's death, I found my son sitting on the sofa. Tears in his eyes, he said, "I miss Dad."

I immediately went into "I can fix this" mode. I asked if he wanted to go to a movie. Did he want McDonalds for dinner? Maybe we could go bowling? I could let him beat me at a video game...? I wanted to do whatever it took to fix it for him.

But he said, "Mom. How about I just sit with this until it goes away on its own?"

I've learned so much from my children. Every day I learn something new. But this particular lesson from my young teen boy had a profound impact on me. I carry it into conversations with clients, with students, and now with you.

When a hard emotion arises, it's okay to sit with it all the way through to completion.

In the last chapter we learned about factors of resilience that can aid us in our grief. I see those as protective factors; preventative pieces that aid us in our grief.

In this next section, I would like to discuss ways to *increase* our resilience by developing healthy coping skills.

While most of my writing is related to grief and how to navigate through the harder parts, this section is directed to any kind of distress and not limited to grief.

My prayer is that it is helpful to you.

Self-Awareness

As I mentioned in the previous chapter, self-awareness is important for resilience and emotional intelligence, but it is also critically important in helping us *cope*. Recognizing and accurately labeling your emotional experience is critical in order to respond to your current state, to self-soothe, and to use that information to move toward a goal.

In my Introduction to Psychology class, when we are discussing the module on "Emotion," I have students take out a piece of paper (or now, an electronic device), and in one minute, write down as many emotion words as they can think of.

I start them out with happiness, interest, anger, fear and disgust (the basic emotions a baby initially shows between 2-4 months of age). I set my timer, and I wait as they brainstorm as many emotion words they know.

I call "time" and I have them count up the number of emotions they were able to name in 60 seconds.

Try it yourself real quick. Go ahead. I'll wait.

How many words did you come up with?

Are you surprised to learn that it's rare to have any one student list more than 15 emotions?

After this exercise, we combine our lists to make a master emotional vocabulary list on the white board, and we categorize the emotion words according to theme and intensity.

For example, the theme of "Interest" might include words like curious, passionate, zealous, excited, attracted, and twitterpated (my favorite word in the movie "Bambi"). The theme of "Anger" might contain words like livid, irate, annoyed, exasperated, and miffed.

What's the point of this exercise? Why would I spend a large portion of valuable class time building a list of emotional vocabulary words for my late adolescent and young adult students?

Because the beginning of communication, the heart of relationships (interpersonal and intrapersonal), the core of self-awareness, requires an ability to accurately name the emotions we experience.

To accurately label your emotions, you must have the words for them. A rich emotional vocabulary is the beginning of strong emotional intelligence and emotional literacy. The accurate label then gives you more control over how to manage the emotion.

The first step that I recommend to my clients and students, in developing self-awareness, is to develop or locate a robust emotional vocabulary. There are lists online, and you can select the emotion words that often experience. Keep this list handy on your fridge or in your journal or as a photo on your phone.

In my grief, I feel so much more than just sadness: empty, bleak, desolate, lost, worried, inadequate, cherished, loved, panicked, deserted, abandoned, exposed, rejected, stunned, elated, joyful, grateful, guilty, tired, defeated, and hopeful.

That list was just from this past week.

The second step in developing self-awareness is mindfulness. Mindfulness is paying attention. Mindfulness is choosing where you will direct your focus, and then sustaining your focus there.

Mindfulness around emotion, then, is choosing to focus on what your body is feeling, what emotion might be stirring there, and accurately labeling it.

One of the habits I developed during Scott's illness was to journal every morning. I had read *The Artist's Way* by Julia Cameron shortly before he was diagnosed, and I was smitten with this idea of "Morning Pages."

Morning Pages is a stream-of-consciousness writing style where you write (on paper, in longhand) three pages of whatever comes to mind. Usually I do it first thing in the morning, but you can do it any time you want. I write before my morning devotions as a way of clearing my head and preparing myself for what God is going to say to me that day.

Morning Pages removes any sort of filter or judgment, without intention of *anyone ever* reading what is written. My only reader is God. I name and process my emotions in my morning pages: Fear. Excitement. Rage. Abandonment. Self-Pity. Giddiness. It all lands there.

Since Scott died, I've filled journal after journal (and I'm the lady who traditionally collects journals, writes in the first three pages, and then abandons them because I either forget about them or feel I've messed them up somehow). Now I write freely as my emotions flood those pages.

Journaling in this way can be an effective method of developing self-awareness. Self-Awareness is a powerful protective factor in our resilience and in our grief journey. Knowing what you are feeling gives you the ability then to self-soothe and to manage your emotion.

Philosophers have known this truth for a very long time. In *Man's Search for Meaning*, Viktor Frankl quotes Spinoza, saying, "Emotion, which is suffering, ceases to be suffering as soon as we form a clear and precise picture of it."

Self-awareness can give us such a clear picture.

Self-Regulation

In the last chapter, I wrote about Self-Regulation as a factor of resilience, but I didn't write about *how* to do this. Some of us struggle with tolerating or regulating our emotions when they arise because we never learned self-soothing strategies.

My son and I were driving home from an event one evening. His emotions were rising to almost a fevered pitch. He missed his dad; he was angry about an unfair teacher at school; he was scared he wouldn't succeed in class because of that teacher. All of these things spiraled upwards to a point of crisis where he was having trouble catching his breath.

I pulled off to the side, put on the hazards, and put the car in park. Then I led him in a grounding technique.

Me: "Take a slow, deep breath. Now, look around and name five things you can see."

Him: (slowly, haltingly) "...Tree, ...grass, ...person on the sidewalk, ...the dashboard, ...glove compartment."

Me: "Now, list four things you can feel."

Him: (touching each thing)"My jacket, ...my jeans, ...the seat, ...the car door."

Me: "List three things you can hear."

Him: "Cars passing by, ...the wind, ...my breath."

Me: "Two things you can smell?"

Him: "Soap from washing my hands. Your perfume."

Me: "Tell me one thing you can taste."

Him: "My tears."

We sat for a while. He breathed. I waited. He asked to go home. He said he felt a little better.

Do you see the pattern? Using all the senses. Five, four, three, two, one.

Sometimes a person in serious distress has to do this process more than once. This grounding technique is useful to calm intense emotions because this gets us out of our head and into our body, our senses; into the moment.

Grounding techniques like this distract the brain's amygdala (the part of the brain that is over-firing and creating hyper-arousal) and pulls energy to another part of the brain that requires the more complex activities of analysis, identification, language, and verbal processing.

Another active way to overcome the body's physical response to intense emotion is to alter the body's reaction to stress or crisis by focusing on TIPP: Temperature, Intense exercise, Paced breathing, and Paired muscle relaxation.

Temperature: We can manage an emotional crisis by lowering our body temperature to actually "chill out." Sucking on an ice cube, putting a cool cloth on your face, or maybe running your hands under cold water could help. I personally like ice cream sandwiches.

Intense exercise: We all know the many benefits of aerobic exercise, but the main goal here is to increase the oxygen to your organs, to slow your heart rate and to regulate your breathing. Intensity is key, and length of the exercise is less important. Running in place, sprinting to your car, jumping jacks in the bathroom at work: whatever it takes to wear you out and to push oxygen out to your body.

Paced breathing: When we are in crisis, our breathing becomes shallow. Our bodies take the lowered oxygen to mean there's a shortage of air, and the brain panics, causing us to gasp for more air, further limiting our oxygen. Feeling short of breath, we then hyperventilate, and the cycle worsens.

Paced breathing counteracts this cycle. There are so many ways to do paced breathing, and I won't tell you that one is better than another. I will tell you that it's important to fill your diaphragm and to exhale what feels like even more air than you took in.

Sometimes it also helps me to recite words or mantras with my breaths. I slowly inhale a positive word like "peace," and exhale the word that is causing me distress, like "fear." There's something about the words flowing in and out that also focuses my mind as I'm calming my breaths.

Paired or progressive relaxation: If you haven't tried this, it's quite therapeutic. It's usually done lying on your back in a comfortable position. Systematically isolate a muscle group (your forehead, for example), and tighten it up. Scrunching and holding the tightness for a moment, you feel the tension, the muscle contraction.

Then release the tension and pay attention to that release. Moving from the top of your head, through the neck, back, arms, trunk, hips, legs, ankles, and feet, isolate, tighten, hold, and release. You are pairing tension and relaxation together, and progressing through the body.

If you are in a place where lying down and relaxing every muscle group isn't feasible, you can still identify the place where you feel tension, and do relaxation to that muscle group.

As I said in the first section, recognizing and labeling emotions is the first task. Self-soothing strategies to calm them is critically important. We become more emotionally intelligent when we are able to tolerate difficult emotions and then shake them off when they have begun to lift.

Lashing out, hurting others, blaming, projecting your distress onto others: these are the opposite of emotional intelligence. By working to identify, self-soothe and tolerate your distress, you will reduce the risk of causing harm to yourself or others.

One of my clients, and I'm sure she's not alone, tells me that once she's in a certain mood, that mood seems to stain everything else she does that day. If she wakes up in a bad mood, she will be in a bad mood until she goes back to bed. She doesn't know how to regulate that mood, and it ends up controlling her.

One strategy that therapists sometimes use is called the "Push Button Technique" that comes out of Adlerian therapy. It's simple enough that it can be done alone without therapeutic guidance.

Read through the instructions before beginning.

1. To begin, get in a comfortable position. Close your eyes and take a deep, cleansing breath. Recall a beautiful memory, one where you feel safe, warm, loved or celebrated. Where were you? Who else was there? What was happening? Pay special attention to how you feel. What emotions are you experiencing in that memory?

2. Open your eyes, take a deep breath, clear that memory from your mind, and close your eyes. This time, recall a hard, difficult, or even painful memory. Where were you? Who else was there? What was happening? Pay special attention to how you feel. What emotions are you experiencing in that memory?

3. Finally, open your eyes, take a deep breath, clear that memory from your mind, and close your eyes again. Go back to a beautiful, happy, pleasant or fun memory. Where were you? Who else was there? What was happening? Pay special attention to how you feel. What emotions are you experiencing in that memory?

This is a technique that allows you to flex between emotions, or even moods, by choosing which memory you will concentrate on.

Therapists find this exercise helps clients see they are not at the whim of their emotions but, instead, they can monitor the interaction between thoughts and feelings. We can create and maintain pleasant or unpleasant feelings of our choice; we are able to quickly interrupt and shift from an unpleasant emotion to a more pleasant one by choosing our thought or memory.

Mental Agility

Now it is time to go deeper into what might be at the core of our distress.

My car was making a really odd noise: insistent, annoying, and embarrassingly loud. I knew that it, like a whiny child, would not get better without purposeful attention, so I made an appointment at the service station for the next morning.

When I arrived, I handed over the keys and told them my concerns, and then asked if there was a shuttle that could bring me to work. Yes, there was a shuttle— a minivan parked right outside with the doors open. The driver was standing at the end of the desk, drinking coffee. He assured me he'd be out in a minute.

When I approached the minivan, I could see there was a very elderly gentleman in the front passenger seat. He had thin hair, a portable oxygen tank in his lap, and age spots on his hands. My eyes moved up to his kind eyes.

In the backseat was a younger man, early 30s. His eyes didn't look so kind. They looked angry. He didn't acknowledge me when I climbed in next to him, as he was very busy on his phone.

The driver finally came out, shut our doors, and hopped in the driver's seat. As soon as we began backing out of the parking spot, the man next to me began muttering under his breath. He would attempt a phone call, not get through, disconnect the call, and cuss under his breath. He'd send a text, and mutter a louder swear word under his breath, and slam his fist down against the bench seat.

By the time we reached the highway, he was no longer muttering. His profanities were loud and bouncing off the interior walls of the van. He was so agitated he was kicking the seat in front of him (the seat where the older man with the oxygen sat) and slamming his elbow against the back of our seat.

The driver pulled off onto the shoulder of the highway, put the van into park, turned around, and looked the man directly in the eye. "I will happily turn this van around, and you can sit at the station until your car is ready. Or you can watch your mouth, and wait your turn to get dropped off. Your choice."

The young man sighed heavily and leaned back in the seat. The driver looked at him a bit longer to make sure the guy was going to behave, and then proceeded to drive back out onto the highway.

I didn't want to, but as a psychotherapist, I felt a professional obligation to help. The man beside me was clearly in distress. "Okay, I don't need to know what's going on, but if you want to tell me, I'll listen."

It turns out he had a meeting that morning at work, and he thought if he got his car dropped off early enough, he'd catch the shuttle with plenty of time to make the meeting.

However, the gentleman in the front seat had checked in first, and our shuttle was bringing him across town to his dialysis appointment. This meant the young man next to me was going to be late for his work meeting. When he finally found out this was the situation, he couldn't reach anyone at work to let them know where he was or why he would be late for his meeting.

Of course, he was frustrated. He had plans and there were obstacles that dropped in front of him that he couldn't have anticipated.

Now, if he'd had some self-awareness, he could have started labeling the emotions he was feelings: perhaps he was experiencing frustration and irritation. Maybe he felt disrespected. Maybe he was embarrassed that he was going to be late to the meeting.

With self-regulation, he could have taken some deep breaths. Maybe he could have noticed five things he could see, four things he could touch, and so on. Perhaps he could have said some things to himself that would help him self-soothe.

But instead, he was agitated and upset, and he reacted with strong behaviors that were alienating, even frightening to those of us trapped in the vehicle with him.

I listened to him. When he finally finished explaining what was going on, I said, "Wow. This is hard. You expected this to go smoothly, and it didn't. You had high expectations."

I know my expectations of this life were high. I expected to live happily ever after with my husband. I expected our marriage to be all butterflies and rainbows. I expected to retire with him and spend our golden years holding hands and watching our grandchildren frolic.

It didn't work out that way for me.

Albert Ellis (1998), a world renowned Cognitive Psychologist, developed a theory called Rational Emotive Behavior Therapy or REBT. (Stay with me here. This is *really* good stuff.)

Ellis suggested that much of our distress occurs when

A) something happens to you (A = Activating event)

B) you hold a fixed thought about it (B = Belief)

C) and you have an emotional reaction to it (C = Consequence)

With the young man in the shuttle:

(A) The activating event was that he planned to make the meeting on time, but that fell through,

(B) He believed life should have gone his way, and

(C) The consequence was that he ended up frustrated and angry.

You see, his distress wasn't caused by the missed meeting, although he thought it was.

We can't control what happens to us or around us. The activating event is outside our control.

Our emotional response is outside of our control, as well. This man was angry, but that was the consequence. Our emotions may *feel* problematic, but our feelings are always a consequence of something else. They are like the rear wheels of a front wheel drive car—they follow along, tracking directly behind whatever is leading them.

The problem within this paradigm resides in B: our beliefs. We can't control what happens to us, and the emotions are a consequence.

The only thing we can control, the only thing that creates the problematic, physiological stress response, is what we *believe*.

Have you heard of "stinking thinking?" It's a phrase originating from Alcoholics Anonymous that describes a thought trap that can lead a person back to drinking. It is descriptive of all sorts of self-destructive ways of thinking. The view holds that we have the power to control what, and how, we think.

Maybe you've heard of the apostle Paul in the New Testament who writes, "We demolish arguments and every pretension that sets itself up against the knowledge of God, and we take captive every thought to make it obedient to Christ" (2 Corinthians 10:5).

Paul understood that our thoughts, regardless of the circumstances, determine our response. He also believed we could capture and alter those thoughts to align them with the truth.

So, here's your job: you can challenge the belief that is irrational. Your belief is causing you pain. You are convinced of a lie that is poisoning how you experience yourself, others, and life in general.

Specifically, there are three irrational beliefs most of us hold that are troublesome. Keep in mind these are irrational; these are lies. These are destructive and damaging.

1) *"I must do well."*

I must be perfect. I must be the best. I must stand out. I must meet others' expectations of me, etc. (The demand is on *me, my* performance, *my* success.)

2) *"You must treat me well."*

You must recognize my importance. You must make accommodations for me. You must see or anticipate my needs and meet them. You must put me first, etc. (The demand is on *you* and *your* recognition of me.)

3) *"Life must be fair."*

Life must be easy. Life must be hassle-free. Life must go the way I planned, etc. (The demand is on *life* meeting my expectations.)

As you look at this list of irrational beliefs, do you see the word that pops out in each item? Do you see the difficult word? This word is at the heart of many of our problems.

Must. "Must' is a really hard word. Very demanding. It suggests a mandate, a necessity, an imperative. I must do well. You must treat me well. Life must be fair, easy, and hassle-free.

But who says? Why must I do well? Where is it written that you must treat me well? Who do you know who has a life that's fair or easy or hassle free?

Look at how this impacted the guy on the shuttle. He felt he must do well. He *had* to be present, on time, and in command for this work meeting. He couldn't look bad. He must be a success.

He demanded that others treat him well. He needed the shuttle driver to see how important he was. He expected the older fellow be late for his medical appointment. He required his co-workers to check their phones and respond to help him solve his problem. Life was supposed to be fair, easy, hassle free.

The difficulties had to go away, or he would grow increasingly hostile and violent.

Oh, I know what you're thinking: "Wow, Dr. Mork, you're right. This *is* good stuff. But what am I supposed to do with this?"

Great question, friend.

Ellis explains that every irrational belief holds a kernel of truth, and that we have to dig out the part that is irrational while holding on to what is true. Instead of demanding these "musts," we can replace them with "preferences."

1) I ~~must~~ *prefer to* do well.
   I prefer doing my best. I would like to stand out. I don't need to meet others' expectations of me, although it'd be nice to please them, etc.

2) ~~You must~~ *I prefer you* treat me well.

I'd like you to see me as important. I hope you will make accommodations for me. I want you to care about my needs and try to meet them. I wish you'd put me first, etc.

3) *I prefer* **life ~~must~~ be fair.**
Life is stressful. Few people have it easy. Life is going to have hassles. I like things to go the way I planned, but I can navigate obstacles pretty well, etc.

Do you see the difference? The altered beliefs are more accurate, reasonable, and attainable. They create permission to falter during hard times and to anticipate setbacks. They allow us to be flexible in how we respond to ourselves and others.

Getting back to the young man in the shuttle. I told him I was teaching about irrational beliefs in a class later that day. I told him about the "musts" that make our lives feel harder because they are so demanding and unyielding. I told him about the ways we can shift our language to "preferences" so we can be a little more patient with ourselves, with others, and with life's hassles and hardships.

Surprisingly, he was pretty receptive. He admitted that he tends to demand a lot from others, and he assumes they will accommodate him. He told me that he and his wife argue a lot because he expects a lot from her, and he gets impatient when he doesn't get his way. (I was thinking, "Really? What a shocker.")

He went quiet for a while, and I left him alone. He stared out the window as we exited off the highway and drove to the dialysis center.

When we stopped in front of the building, he jumped out of the van, opened the front passenger door for the older man, helped him out, and carried the man's oxygen tank while he slowly walked the gentleman into the building.

The young man's disposition was different when he got back in the van: instead of anxious and angry, he was now calm and chatty.

This skill is a game changer, my friend. When you feel yourself getting stressed, ask yourself what the underlying demand is. What is the ultimatum you are setting up for yourself? What's the unrealistic expectation? What is the "must" that is creating an unattainable paradox for you?

Rehearsing the new preference is critically important: using the words "I prefer; I don't demand" repeatedly throughout the day helps develop new neurological connections in your brain. As you rehearse them, the new language become a habit.

The shuttle driver dropped the young man off at work. He'd missed the meeting but seemed fine with it. I made it to class on time.

Later that day, the service station called to tell me what the problem was with my car and what it would cost to repair.

Then he paused. He said, "The shuttle driver came back this morning and told us what happened. We are really grateful you helped de-escalate that situation. Our manager is throwing in a free oil change for you this afternoon to show our appreciation."

See? Albert Ellis got me a free oil change. I told you he was good.

Goal Setting

The latin word *finis* can mean one of a few different things. *Finis* can mean finish, the end. But *finis* can also mean a purpose or a goal to be reached.

When we are navigating through the grief process, it may be necessary to set goals in our grief. What is it you need to accomplish?

I know, this seems like an odd concept. I'm sure you're staring at the previous paragraph and wondering "What do you mean, lady? 'Set goals? What do I need to accomplish?' Are you nuts? I just want to feel better."

Goal-setting is fundamental work in grief, though. Without direction, we can get stuck and feel aimless and unmotivated.

When you think about your grief work, what do you want to achieve?

How do you want to show up?

What could you learn?

When you look back over your grief journey in a few years, what is it you want to be able to say about it?

As a psychotherapist, I know that I cannot assign an objective to you. I can't tell you what goal you must target. Only you can identify what your grief goal might be right now.

There are a number of therapeutic techniques that psychologists and counselors use to help clients establish goals.

Don't forget, the goal of grief is *not* to get our loved one back. The goal of grief is *not* to "get over it," "walk away," "move on," or "find closure."

Let me explore a few ways we can begin to identify your goals.

Think of a problem that is related to your loss or your grief. Is it finances? Is it a fractured relationship in the family? Are you in conflict with in-laws? Is it household burdens? Is it trouble in parenting?

The first question I want you to ask yourself is, "How would my life be different if, all of a sudden, I didn't have that problem anymore?"

Think about this for a moment. Indulge in the possibility of the problem being gone. Explore the feeling of freedom. What would it be like for the problem to disappear?

Perhaps you might consider this: imagine you woke up tomorrow and your life felt somehow better, lighter, easier, or fixed. What would be the *first sign* you would notice that something wonderful had happened?

When you think of that first sign, what can you do right now to make that first sign a reality?

Each one of us reading this is going to have a very different answer to this. I am reluctant to offer an example because I don't want to steal away your response.

By exploring what the *first* thing would be that you'd notice, you begin to think in terms of small steps you can take to create a new reality.

This doesn't always mean the source of the problem is gone. Your loved one is still dead. But maybe the kitchen sink is fixed. You greet your sister with openness and warmth instead of suspicion and dread and your relationship begins to mend.

Using this strategy to get you exploring the problem, ask yourself this: "What is the first step that I can take to make this problem go away?"

I'm not a fan of fortune telling, but here is a fairly harmless question that can be a helpful way of discovering your own goal for your grief work: "Imagine that there is a special kind of crystal ball in front of you: it allows you to see yourself in the future. Notice that you can see the kind of future that you want for yourself, the kind of future where things work out for you. As you look into this crystal ball, what does that 'future you want' look like?"

This question can get my heart pounding really hard. What does the "future I want" look like?

I'm starting to live it. The future I want is a future where I can use what I know and share it with others. I can write, and speak, and teach on grief and humor, and I can help someone else.

What does *your* future look like?

Once we identify our goal for grief work, here are a few tools to reach that goal.

Acting As If: Have you ever heard the saying, "Fake it 'til you make it?" It feels somewhat inauthentic, but there's something therapeutically valuable about acting out a new behavior as though it comes naturally to you. Sometimes a professional counselor might ask you to "act as if" you are already the person you would like to be.

Think of it: if you were acting as if you were the person you want to be, what would be different about you?

If you were acting like the person you want to be, and a friend you hadn't seen in months (or years, if it requires a slow change) saw you, what would they see as different?

If there was a video of the "new" you, what would you first notice about yourself? What might be some initial indicators that could show you that you are headed in the right direction?

Taking those answers, can you begin acting as if you've reached the goal?

Catching Yourself: Even when we are acting "as if," we will still slip into old habits and behaviors. It's so important to see when we are falling and to isolate the particular behaviors that contribute to the problem.

Here's an example in my own life. Please, I am being vulnerable here and humbly ask that you not judge me harshly. I understand there is an expectation that, as a helper, as a mental health professional, I should have complete mastery over my own behaviors. That is a very high expectation of anyone, as we are all flawed and fall short of perfection.

I struggle with compulsive binge-eating. When I say I struggle, I mean I fight it, I wrestle and engage in knock-down-drag-out skirmishes with it.

The pattern is this: I stop at the store on my way home from work to get food to cook for dinner. I throw favorite snack foods in the cart, thinking the kids will enjoy them, and we're running low. I move through the evening well: dinner, cleaning up the dishes, hanging out with the kids, moving into bedtime routines.

Then they say goodnight, and I lock the doors. I turn out the lights. I adjust the thermostat.

Then it happens. There is a gravitational pull to the kitchen. I feel myself walking, against my own will, down the hallway, past the front entrance, through the living room, and into the kitchen. I tell myself, "Not tonight, Melissa. Don't do this to yourself tonight."

But my mind seems to be split—as much as I don't want to do this, there is a stronger force pushing me to get out the snacks I'd bought earlier that day.

This feels so shameful. I feel so embarrassed. I despise myself for losing the battle.

After I've binged, I clean up the refuse. I throw away the wrappers and packages. I carry the garbage out to the garage, tuck it under other trash, go back in the house, close the door behind me, and survey the room to make sure there's no evidence left behind.

I resent myself for being so weak. I walk back to my room, turning off lights. I go to bed.

Tomorrow it might happen again.

If you look through this pattern, you might see your own behavioral pattern emerging. The pattern of drinking, gambling, online shopping, pornography, etc. The pattern tends to be the same for many compulsive or addictive behaviors: the trigger, the isolation, the routine, the shame.

So, let's look at the idea of "catching oneself." We often catch ourselves too late, and the pattern has already begun. As I'm saying, "Not tonight, Melissa. Don't do this to yourself tonight," it's already too late. It's already too late when I'm adjusting the thermostat.

To catch oneself, we need to anticipate when the problem might arise and take steps to avoid the triggers we know are related to the problem.

For me, I catch myself when I don't buy the snack foods. If I do buy them, I give them to the kids as soon as I get home.

I can also catch myself right before the final trigger—by knowing my pattern, I can set up an alternative, more pleasing and indulgent behavior that will be equally nourishing to me.

I know that when I'm engaging in this habit, I'm tired, I'm worn out, I haven't done much for me all day, I'm looking for a reward or an endorphin rush. I also know I'm too tired to exercise, and it's too late to call a friend. While they are great solutions, I'd be unlikely to do them.

To catch myself, I recognize my triggers and make a list of the things I can do instead. As I turn down the thermostat, I have a new plan of action that takes me in the opposite direction from the kitchen.

I can watch comedy on my laptop in my bedroom. I can take a long, hot bath. I can read a good book. Sometimes I can tell myself, "Lie down in bed for ten minutes. If you still need to eat, you can do it then." Usually I'm asleep before the ten minutes have passed.

In grief, sometimes we engage in maladaptive behaviors like this as a way of coping. Binging on food, drinking, shopping too much, and numbing ourselves with other things: we develop poor or even destructive habits or addictions.

The problem is that we aren't actually helping our grief. Instead we are left with two problems: the grief *and* the consequences the addiction brings.

"Acting as if" I don't have the problem and "catching myself:" both of these are tools that can help us see how life can be and take steps to make it a reality.

Focusing On Solutions: Sometimes our problem is already solved, but we don't hold on to it, or we lose track of the solution. Still, the strategy to solve the problem is already inside of us.

Ask yourself, "When has this *not* been a problem? Are there times when the problem doesn't occur? Are there times, even now, when some of the solution is already occurring? Can I do more of what's working?"

Another way of finding a solution is to externalize the problem. Externalizing the problem can lend profound insight in finding the solutions. Here's what I mean:

Let's say you are arguing with your siblings over your parents' belongings, and you blame the siblings for the conflict, for being greedy and for not appreciating you. Externalizing the problem means separating the problem from the people who are affected by the problem. Give the problem a name. In this example, it's Blame. "How is Blame stopping me from reaching a solution?" How is Blame affecting me?" "What is Blame whispering in my ear?"

This will not change how your siblings act toward you, but it will change the way you see them. Your siblings are not inherently bad people. They have loved you, and you have loved them.

Insistently, repeatedly tell yourself that the people and the problem are not fused together. The problem has an agenda to destroy your relationships. The problem needs to be dismantled. The people do not.

Empowerment: In Feminist therapy, where much of the focus is on empowerment and strength, therapists will often ask, "What is the most powerful thing you can do right now?"

This may feel unsettling, particularly if you are a woman and you have been celebrated for your meekness and submission. Women, especially, are not encouraged to consider where we might be powerful. Men have also been culturally curtailed in demonstrating any form of power outside of physical strength and sexual prowess.

But maybe we can consider "power" in a different context. Think of the power in the engine of a car. In that context, power means "effective in moving you forward."

What's the most influential, impactful thing you can do right now? What is the one thing that will allow you to move toward your goal?

Here's the most profound and transformative experience in my grief process following my mother's death, and it was directly related to this question of "What's the most powerful thing I can do?"

My mother was killed in a car crash my junior year of college. She stopped at a stop sign, looked for traffic across the four-lane highway she was crossing, and proceeded to cross.

A semi driver, coming around a curve at high speeds, traversed all four lanes of the highway and collided with her van, pushing her vehicle into the far ditch.

Had he stayed in his lane he would not have made contact with her van, and she would have safely gone on her way. To this day, we are unclear as to what happened. We did not seek an autopsy, my father did not want to pursue a lawsuit against the driver or the trucking company. Even now, my siblings and I have no answers.

But after the crash, with no answers, my anger and resentment toward the driver and the trucking company was tangible. When I would see their trucks on the road, I would have to fight myself not to give the drivers the middle finger. I refused to shop at stores that used their company to deliver goods. I despised the driver.

For ten years, I was angry. I carried my anger for that driver and that trucking company for ten horrible years, and it ate away at me.

As I approached the ten-year anniversary, I was teaching a class on various therapies, and this question from Feminist

Therapy stared at me out of the book I was reading. "What is the most powerful thing you can do right now?"

I dreaded the answer: "Forgive him."

I didn't want to. This driver had killed my mother. Her death caused my father to die from a broken heart.

I was orphaned while still in college because of this man. My parents weren't there to help me navigate adulthood. They weren't there for my pregnancies and miscarriages. They weren't there when my babies were born. My parents weren't there to see me get my master's degree or my doctorate or become a professor.

They weren't there, and I blamed that truck driver.

Forgive him? Seriously?

But the whisper grew louder.

What's the most powerful thing I can do?

Forgive him.

Just forgive him.

You have to forgive him.

On the tenth anniversary of the crash, which would also have been my father's birthday (did I mention she died on his birthday?), I called the highway patrol in the town where she'd died, and explained who I was and the information I needed.

With the man's name and phone number scribbled on the back of a used envelope, I hung up and said a prayer.

Then I dialed his number.

Thankfully he didn't answer, and I was able to leave a voicemail.

"Hi. You don't know me. My name is Melissa. Ten years ago today, you were involved in a collision that caused my mother's death. I am calling to tell you that I am choosing to forgive you. I am sorry you were involved in that event, and I pray you have found, or will find, forgiveness for yourself. If you want to connect to talk about this further, my number is...."

This was completely, unquestionably, God-inspired and led. I couldn't have done this for myself.

I felt so much freer after disconnecting from that phone call. What was the most powerful thing I did? I released *me* from the anger and pain I was carrying.

This may have had no impact on this man. Maybe he never heard that message. I don't know. I never heard back from him. I didn't need to. The act of forgiveness empowered me to move forward in freedom.

Anne Lamott says, "Not *forgiving* is like drinking *rat poison* and then waiting for the rat to die."

I forgave the rat for my benefit. I didn't do this for the rat.

What's the most powerful thing you can do right now? Sometimes you are empowered to take action. Perhaps the most powerful thing you can do is remain silent. Your most powerful action might be to do nothing.

Maybe the most powerful thing you can do is to pray. To forgive. To grieve.

Ultimately, all of these suggestions throughout this chapter are meant to bring you to a goal of healing or personal strength.

I hope when you've met your goal, you can say you arrived with integrity, that you expressed your emotions honestly, that you sought support when you needed it, that you loved those around you well.

Finis

Humor

I know, I know. You reached this chapter and thought, "Finally! I've been waiting to laugh, woman!"

Sorry to disappoint, but as I said at the outset, I'm an educator, not an entertainer. I don't consider myself all that funny.

I *am* a Certified Humor Professional (CHP). But even this label doesn't guarantee I'll be funny.

The CHP is a designation through the Association for Applied and Therapeutic Humor (AATH). A person working toward this certification will complete a three-year, college-level set of courses through the Humor Academy (HA), investigating the value of humor in a number of domains. We study ways humor can be used effectively in areas like healthcare, therapy, teaching, and leadership.

At the completion of our studies, we each complete a humor related project in our professional field that we must present at an annual conference. My project was on the correlations between parenting styles in family of origin, emotional intelligence, and humor styles in college students.

When the three years of study are done and the project is successfully completed and presented, the person may earn the designation of Certified Humor Professional. There are fewer than 100 of us around the world.

Being a Certified Humor Professional means I have studied humor.

I'm the academic, not the comic.

When I began writing this book, I was excited about incorporating a few themes from my humor studies into a conversation about grief, but when I'd talk about it, some folks were skeptical. They wondered if I would trivialize the topic of grief by making light of it, by cracking jokes about death.

The connotations of the word *humor* can be quite narrow, I'm afraid. We think humor relates only to jokes and riddles, stand-up comics and situational comedies. But there is so much more to good humor than this.

My friend, Janet, who carries joy with her like a bright yellow umbrella, who exudes enthusiasm for every person in her presence, and who laughs and giggles her way through every casual conversation, will say, "Melissa, I just don't have a sense of humor. I can't tell a joke to save my life."

Yet, based on what *I* see as good humor, I would argue that Janet is a woman with the very best sense of humor.

There is bad humor out there. Jokes aimed at race, ethnicity, (dis)ability, age, gender, sexual orientation, political party, or another people group is risky humor. The highly sexualized joke is not safe humor. Ridicule, which is an aggressive humor targeting another person, is not good humor when it inflicts harm on another.

There is a *lot* of healthy humor, however. Good humor could involve a joke, light teasing, a pun or play on words. We might find it in situations, conversations, playful banter, or improvisational interactions. Good humor can even be dark, if it helps the person regain control in intense, heavy situations.

Good humor is choosing an attitude of levity and mirth. Most of us are drawn to the person in our friend group or extended family who can bring lightness and laughter to the conversation.

You want to sit next to the person at work who can make the meeting fun, even if by quietly writing funny comments in the margins of the minutes as the meeting drones on and on.

Good humor embraces other positive traits and habits, too. For our purposes here, I am defining a person with good humor as optimistic, full of gratitude, seeking light, looking for beauty.

The person with good humor is able to shift his or her focus, when necessary, onto the good and away from the difficult. This perfectly describes my joy-filled, enthusiastic, laughing friend, Janet.

As I mentioned at the beginning of this book:

Finally, brothers and sisters, whatever is true, whatever is noble, whatever is right, whatever is pure, whatever is lovely, whatever is admirable—if anything is excellent or praiseworthy—think about such things and the God of peace will be with you (Philippians 4:8).

The ability to think about those things is at the heart of good humor.

A few years ago, my church asked me to give a special lecture on suffering during Holy Week. I provided a fairly somber lecture. As part of the discussion, I talked about my own illness.

I've mentioned already that I have an autoimmune disorder. It causes chronic bleeding ulcers and high inflammation of the digestive tract. It can be excruciatingly painful. For years, my disease was barely managed with surgeries, steroids, and other medications, and it has been a significant, often debilitating issue since my early 20's.

The most effective treatment that I have found for my disease is Remicade, a medication infusion I receive at the hospital every six weeks. This medicine is a tumor necrosis factor protein, and, I am not kidding here, the protein is extracted from live mice.

Yes. I am being pumped full of live mouse protein.

FYI, dear reader, I have a mortal fear of rodents. I couldn't watch the movie "Ratatouille" with my children in the theater because the animation was too realistic. "Mouse Hunt?" Could not watch it. I sat turned away from the screen with my eyes clamped shut through the entire movie.

Tom and Jerry cartoons are awful. Tom is fine. Jerry freaks me out.

The presence of a dead mouse in my backyard in the summertime keeps me inside until the following spring. Brightly colored mouse-shaped cat toys make me nervous. Mickey Mouse walking towards me at Disneyland causes me mild angst.

Yet here I am, every six weeks, lying in a hospital bed for a few hours, getting mouse proteins dripped into my veins.

How do they extract this particular tumor necrosis protein?

I'd like to imagine the donor mice reclining in little plasma donation chairs, hooked up to miniscule PICC lines, nibbling on crackers, tiny cups of orange juice nearby with miniature paper straws; the mice flipping through wee little magazines or listening to music with petite earbuds. Every one of them taking a break out of their busy days, generously donating their blood proteins for my survival.

I should also mention the odd side effects of this medication extracted from live mice: I crave cheese, I'm afraid of my cats, I scurry along walls, and I poop behind the stove.

I'm kidding.

I'm not afraid of my cats.

As I stood in front of the church, behind the lectern, somberly sharing about suffering, I told of my struggle with this disease and the miracle of this medication that keeps me alive. The audience graciously laughed at the mildly funny bits.

Scott was in the audience. This is the first time he'd ever heard me speak. We'd been married 20+ years at that point. Afterwards, he came up to hug me, and then he said the following six words to me:

"I didn't know you were funny."

He sat through a thirty-minute presentation on suffering, he heard people laugh, and he was surprised.

But the thing is, we laughed together a lot in our marriage. He'd tell me jokes he'd heard at work. I would tell him funny stories that had happened in my day. He would improvise silly scenarios. I'd make some mindless gaffe that make him smile. He'd tease me. We'd goof off. We would play. We were playful.

But because I didn't tell jokes like he did, he didn't think of me as *funny*.

Is humor restricted to just telling jokes? What makes something (or someone) funny to you?

In this section, I want to discuss some of the facets of humor, the profound value of good humor, and how we can use humor to tolerate our suffering.

Humor—Mirth—Laughter

When researchers study the therapeutic benefits of laughter and humor, they tend to examine three specific divisions:

The stimulus—what is funny? (humor)

The physical reaction or behavior (laughter)

The emotional response—how does it feel? (mirth)

Here's an example of a joke Scott told me:

I was at the ATM today and an old lady asked me to help her check her balance.

So I pushed her over.

Did you find that funny? Researchers could examine why or why not.

Was there a moral violation? Did it feel hostile? Did it seem ageist to you? If that's the case, you might not like the joke.

Maybe you'd heard it before. If the joke doesn't contain some sort of surprise, it won't strike you as funny.

Perhaps there was no incongruity. You already thought the word "balance" referred to her vestibular sense and not her bank account. If that was the case, you wouldn't find the joke funny.

Researchers would be looking at the facets of the humor in that joke. They'd want to know what was happening in one's thought processes when one thinks something is funny. Were you surprised? Were you expecting one ending so the other ending caught you off guard?

So much of what we laugh at is unscripted, unrehearsed, improvisational, situational, conversational, or relational. It's affiliative and, usually, surprising.

A dog went to a telegram office and wrote: "Woof. Woof. Woof. Woof. Woof. Woof. Woof. Woof. Woof." The clerk examined the paper and told the dog: "There are only nine words here. You could send another 'Woof' for the same price." "But," the dog replied, "that would make no sense at all."

If you found that joke truly funny, you will have exhibited some sort of behavioral manifestation of it. You smiled or nodded. Maybe you breathed a quick breath out your nose or you actually chuckled. Some humor will lift your spirits but not manifest in laughter.

Based on votes from 2 million people across 70 countries, here is the funniest joke in the world, according to The University of Hertfordshire and the British Association for the Advancement of Science:

> *A couple of New Jersey hunters are out in the woods when one of them falls to the ground. He doesn't seem to be breathing and his eyes have rolled back in his head. The other guy whips out his mobile phone and calls the emergency services. He gasps to the operator: "My friend is dead! What can I do?" The operator, in a soothing voice, says: "Just take it easy. I can help. First, let's make sure he's dead." There is a silence, then a shot is heard. The guy's voice comes back on the line. He says: "OK, now what?*

I know. It's pretty dark.

Still, if you found that funny, you might have noticed a bit of a lift in your chest (mirth). Whenever you encounter something you find funny, you may feel lightened or cheered, often with a noticeable change in mood. "Mirth" is the emotional experience of encountering something funny.

Mirth is that event most of us are seeking when we are looking for humor. We aren't in search of a cognitive event of surprise or incongruity. We are looking for the levity, the emotional lift.

Be clear that these are all different things. Humor is what we *think* is funny, laughter is what we *do* in response to what we found funny, and mirth is what we *feel* when we think something is funny.

Physical Benefits of Laughter

"The arrival of a good clown into a village does more for its health than 20 asses laden with drugs," Thomas Sydenham (English physician, 1624-1689).

Proverbs 17:22, "A merry heart is like good medicine."

How can I convince you that laughter is good for you? Well, let's start with this: the benefits of laughter are similar to the physical benefits of aerobic exercise. For example, 10-15 minutes of daily laughing can burn up to forty calories. Laughing one hundred times can burn as many calories as ten minutes on a stationary bike. After a good long hearty laugh, your muscles will remain relaxed for up to forty-five minutes.

Do you need more evidence than that?

Okay, how about this? Laughter activates the mesolimbic dopaminergic reward system. It has been shown to increase endorphins that decrease the experience of pain and increase pain tolerance.

Still want more? Okay, buckle in.

In the field of psychoneuroimmunology, the field that explores the interactions between the immune system and the nervous system, Dr. Lee Berk and his co-researchers studied fifty-two healthy men who viewed an hour-long, humorous video. Researchers drew blood ten minutes before the video, half an hour into the video, half an hour after watching the video, and then twelve hours after that.

Berk and friends found that humor reduced the stress hormone cortisol and catecholamine levels in the body. Humor also increased the production of antibodies that bolster the immune system.

Dr. Michael Miller and associates found that laughter is linked to healthy function of blood vessels. While it seems to be common knowledge that psychological distress can impact blood vessel function to the point of possibly causing cholesterol buildup in the arteries, Dr. Miller found that laughter was related to vasodilation (the veins dilating) and increased blood flow.

In 1964, Norman Cousins developed a crippling, horrifically painful collagen disease of the connective tissues called Ankylosing Spondylitis, which couldn't be treated well with medical interventions of the time. His survival prognosis was 1 in 500. The specialist admitted he'd not personally seen anyone outlive it.

Having read a book by Hans Selye (the theorist behind the Fight or Flight stress response) called *The Stress of Life*, Mr. Cousins remembered having learned about harmful consequences of negative emotion on physiology.

Mr. Cousins wondered, "If negative emotions produce negative chemical changes in the body, wouldn't positive emotions produce positive chemical changes? Is it possible that love, hope, faith, laughter, confidence, and the will to live have therapeutic value? Do chemical changes occur only on the downside?"

As a side note, Mr. Cousins confronted an issue in his book that I want to discuss at length elsewhere but will address briefly here. We have become a culture terrified of pain. We do everything we can to avoid it; we medicate ourselves against it; and in my humble opinion, it is the fear of pain that has caused the opioid crisis in our country. We demand to be anesthetized from all pain at all times. Even in the '60s, when Cousins wrote his book, we were a culture that fled from pain.

Mr. Cousins admitted that he had to adjust his frame of mind around pain; he could endure it if he *knew* it would lead toward healing. In the next chapter, I will explore this concept as it relates to grief.

Mr. Cousins made a therapeutic decision to pursue positive emotions. He writes that he "began the part of the program calling for the full exercise of the affirmative emotions as a factor in enhancing body chemistry. It was easy enough to hope and love and have faith, but what about laughter?"

If you've been in the hospital, you know there aren't a lot of laughs. If you're in excruciating pain, it's hard to find mirth. Being in pain, in the hospital, and alone? That is a serious downer.

Here's what Norman Cousins did. Remember this was in the 1960s, so these shows might not be familiar to you. With the help of Allen Funt, who produced the classic "Candid Camera" television show, Mr. Cousins was given reels of Candid Camera, Marx Brothers movies, a projector, and a screen.

In his hospital room, he watched these very funny clips. He writes:

I made the joyous discovery that ten minutes of genuine belly laughter had an anesthetic effect and would give me at least two hours of pain-free sleep. When the pain-killing effect of the laughter wore off, we would switch on the motion picture projector again, and, not infrequently, it would lead to another pain-free sleep interval.

Read that again: ten minutes of laughter gave him two hours of *pain free* sleep.

But that's not all, folks. Wait! There's more!

This practice did more than give him comfort. His focus on positive emotions like faith, hope, and love, along with his pursuit of laughter, had some peculiar medical benefits. Somehow his body began to fight the inflammation that was destroying his connective tissues.

After every laughter episode, the medical staff would measure his sedimentation rates. They found a drop of a least five points. Each drop didn't seem statistically significant when looked at as an isolated event.

However, each five-point drop would hold and thus they became cumulative. "I was greatly elated by the discovery that there is a physiologic basis for the ancient theory that laughter is good medicine."

There was one problem with this treatment strategy, though. His laughing was too loud and was disturbing the other patients. He had to move out of the hospital and into a hotel.

Cousins was delighted to discover his living arrangements dropped in price by two thirds, and he could sleep without being awakened by doctors' rounds, sponge baths, blood draws, or other annoying hospital routines. Cousins believed this all helped his recovery, too.

Quoting Proverbs 17:22, "A merry heart is like good medicine," Mr. Cousins concluded,

Some people, in the grip of uncontrollable laughter, say their ribs are hurting. The expression is probably accurate, but it is a delightful "hurt" that leaves the individual relaxed almost to the point of an open sprawl. It is the kind of "pain," too, that most people would do well to experience every day of their lives. It is as specific and tangible as any other form of physical exercise. Though its biochemical manifestations have yet to be as explicitly charted and understood as the effects of fear or frustration or rage, they are real enough.

My friends, Mr. Cousins was prophetic in his statement. There is so much research being conducted now on the physiological benefits of humor and laughter.

What I can conclude from humor research is that laughter really is the best medicine (except for treating diarrhea).

Social Benefits of Laughter and Humor

Have you ever been in an argument with a loved one, and you're growing more and more annoyed by the conflict? Then the other person says something self-deprecating or gently teases you about something. Even if you don't laugh, the attempt at humor lowers your anxiety and softens the conflict.

In a research study on the use of humor in negotiations, Maemura & Horita (2012) report "a conscious grasp and efficient use of humor can be used to encourage better negotiation practices by helping negotiations explore new issues, break out of deadlocks, and prevent circular argumentation."

We know, intuitively, that humor brings great social benefits. We are drawn to others who are funny. When we are around someone who can bring lightness to the conversation, we are more apt to listen. Humor helps persuade us in arguments and sells us on another way of seeing things. This is why so many commercials are funny.

In the classroom, I find my students are drawn to humor. If I tell a fun story related to the content, they seem to remember the content better. A professor's use of humor reduces anxiety and the feeling that this is "high stakes" learning. Laughter allows students to relax, which enhances learning and recall (Berk, 2001).

If I talk about my mistakes and laugh, I let them to see that I'm human. I'm giving them permission to make mistakes and to laugh at themselves, as well. Self-deprecating humor lowers the power differential, so I'm less the "sage on the stage" and more a person who is facilitating their learning and cheering them on.

In the workplace, humor is extremely valuable. People who can effectively use humor at work are seen as more credible and in control (even when they aren't).

Humor is an equalizer, as it brings people together. When supervisors use humor, subordinates show increased work performance, rate their experience as more positive, rate their supervisors higher, and feel more connected (Mesmmer-Magnus, Glew, & Viswesvaran, 2012).

A few years ago, I went on sabbatical from both teaching and from seeing patients at the clinic. It had been a difficult season for me: I was suffering burnout and compassion fatigue from doing therapy with some difficult clients. I had some serious issues from my autoimmune disorder that required surgical correction. As a consequence of the many years of Prednisone to treat my disease, I had grown morbidly obese.

I sat at home most days of that sabbatical, recovering from surgery, working on weight loss, and studying humor. I was alone with the dog, and my husband was at work, my children were at school, my colleagues were teaching, and my friends were all gainfully employed. With all that bustling activity out there going on without me, I sat in my chair or walked on the treadmill, reading dry research on humor.

By the way, as I studied humor, I found E. B. White's quote quite accurate: "Analyzing humor is like dissecting a frog. Few people are interested and the frog dies of it."

I decided I needed levity in my life, so I chose to take breaks from reading the research to watch funny shows. I selected late-night talk shows, stand-up comics, sitcoms, rom-coms, Vine. I was desperate for a laugh.

But here's what surprised me: No matter how funny the material, I still wasn't laughing. Only when my husband got home from work, my children got off the bus, my friends stopped by, only then did I laugh.

Research has shown that we are thirty times more likely to laugh when we are with others than by ourselves.

However, they don't have to be physically present for us to laugh with them.

We are able to engage in laughter with someone through a virtual medium, too. We know this because we do so much laughing via text and online (Ha!; LOL = laugh out loud; ROFL = rolling on floor laughing; ROTFLSHMSFOAIDMT = rolling on the floor laughing so hard my sombrero fell off and I dropped my taco [used by my friend, Michael Fournier]).

Laughter has so many social benefits. Laughter is like an emollient in conversations. It can reduce tension; it can soften words; it can indicate to the other person that you are open and non-threatening.

Most laughter in those situations is free-floating. It's not tied to a joke or even specific content, and when someone later asks you what you were laughing about, you won't be able to recall. This is called affiliative humor.

Humor is a very social phenomenon. The number one cause for laughter isn't hearing funny jokes. It's the presence of another person.

One of the greatest benefits is that we can use laughter to signal to each other that we are happy, or content, or nervous.

For my kids and me, laughter signalled that we still had a future.

That last day, the day Scott was dying, his breathing changed. Maybe you know that sound. Slowly, throughout the day, the death rattle became stronger.

Around six o'clock that night, I sent the kids down to the cafeteria with their uncle to get dinner. As soon as they left the room, Scott's breathing changed again.

At 6:15, he opened his eyes, looked up, and he exhaled. His breathing just... stopped.

My children were called back up, and we stood there, just the three of us, in stunned silence. It felt like all the air had been sucked out of the room.

They each said to him, "I love you, Daddy." I kissed him goodbye.

We drove home. Holding our breath, saying nothing. We walked into the house, and it was there that I held my kids to me.

We began to weep. Wordless laments. Choking sobs. Gasping cries. Terrifying despair.

We were so afraid of the pain, of our grief, of what this scary future now held for us.

And then, unexpectedly, my daughter, said something that struck us as *funny.*

Out of the blue—we were laughing!

Choking, gasping, breathless sobs morphed into choking, gasping, breathless laughter.

There is no other way to describe it: there was undeniable life in that laughter. We inhaled. There was oxygen. There was breath.

I know what you might be thinking: Wasn't that too soon? To be laughing with your kids when he had just died?

My answer to that is NO. That laughter was just in time.

It was in the laughter that we knew we'd get through this. I heard my children's laughter and I knew they would be fine. They heard my laughter and they knew I would be strong.

It was in that laughter that we signaled to each other that were going to be okay.

Humor and laughter give us powerful social signals.

Intimacy

Humor improves romance. Men are drawn to a woman who laughs, especially if he is the one who is able to make her laugh. He doesn't want her laughing *at* him, but he wants to be perceived as funny and to bring out her laughter.

Women are also drawn to a partner who has a good sense of humor and who is able to make her laugh. Just ask anyone who is currently on an online dating site how often they see "I'm a funny guy" or "I like to laugh" or "A good sense of humor is a must." or "I'm looking for someone to laugh with."

People aren't listing, "I want to marry someone who is smoking hot." They are looking for something sustainable, that will last the lifetime—'til death do us part. Beauty fades. A good sense of humor lasts across the years.

Intimacy is built through laughter. In a study at Oxford by Gray, Parkinson, and Dunbar, (2015), research participants watched either a stand-up comedy clip, a golf instruction video, or a nature documentary. The results found people were more likely to share intimate details about themselves when they were laughing.

One of the more thorough, fun, and interesting marriage researchers of our time is John Gottman. He and his colleague, Robert Levenson, developed an apartment research location dubbed the "Love Lab." In their ongoing research, couples are invited in and their interactions are studied.

During routine, daily conversations, but especially during conflict, researchers watch the couples' facial expressions, eye rolls, smiles, but they also measure heart rate, blood pressure, galvanic skin response, even psychomotor agitation through a pad under their seat called a "jiggleometer."

Gottman and his crew invite newlyweds, old-timers, and everyone in between to participate. Folks in long-term, successful relationships are often referred to as the masters of relationship, while those who are headed for divorce can be referred to as disasters.

Based on the patterns of conflict and conflict resolution they observed, Gottman and his fellow researchers are able to predict with very high rates of accuracy who will be masters and who will be the disasters in marriage.

In past research, Gottman and colleagues have found that using humor during marital conflict is essential to healthy long-term relationships, and humor is predictive of both marital stability and marital satisfaction. Humor and affection were clearly present in stable, happily married couples.

Gottman often talks about "bids" in a relationship. A bid is an attempt by one person to make a connection. He or she is seeking attention, affirmation, affection. A bid might be simple, like a smile, a tickle, a pat on the butt. It might be more complex, like a request for help or an initiation of a conversation.

An example of a bid could be: "The neighbor is mowing his lawn." This comment is a bid for connection, and the other partner might respond positively with, "What's he wearing this time?" or "Ask him to mow ours, too," or even giving the bid a simple thumbs-up.

The content of the response doesn't matter. It's just important that there *is* a response. This response to the bid is called "turning towards" the other person.

To miss a bid or to reject it is "turning away." Sometimes you're just not paying attention; sometimes you're thinking about something else, or you didn't hear it.

Sometimes, turning away from a bid is hostile, like, "Why are you telling me this?" or "Don't you have anything better to do than watch the neighbor?"

In many cases, we turn away because there is a rip or tear in the relationship that isn't repaired.

In a 2004 study, Driver and Gottman observed newlyweds in both a ten-minute conversation over dinner and in a fifteen-minute conflict. They found that the husband played a significant role in both daily interactions and in conflict—specifically with playful bids.

In daily interactions, the husband's ability to initiate playful bids increases the wife's playfulness and her enthusiasm, and his playful bids increase her affection for him. When the husband initiates playfulness, both the husband and wife are able to access humor during conflict.

In class, when we discuss this research, I encourage my students to remember this. How hard is it to turn toward a playful bid? To smile, to wink back, or to giggle. This is the behavioral key that unlocks long-term marital satisfaction—he makes a playful bid, and she smiles.

If you've watched two friends at a coffee shop, you'll see mirror neurons at work. As their conversation flows, the two people unintentionally copy each other in posture, gestures, and facial expressions.

We see mirror neurons at work especially in deep connection, in empathic conversations. When we sit with someone who is crying, we reflect their countenance.

When we share a laugh with someone, we unconsciously mimic their face, their posture. When we are laughing together, we are also reflecting that hormonal and neuronal activity, indicating deep connection.

No wonder so many women list humor highest on attractiveness traits when seeking a spouse. That's hot.

Humor in Adversity

In 2012, I was invited to apply for a sabbatical at my University, and I knew exactly what I wanted to study. As a grief counselor, I saw how precious laughter was in therapy sessions. I wanted to learn about the value of humor in hard times.

In preparation for narrowing the topic, I had been reading a lot about the psychology of humor. There was a preconference event in San Diego with the Society of Personality and Social Psychology (SPSP) on that very topic, Psychology of Humor, and I was thrilled to attend.

Because I found the topic so interesting, I anticipated that this event would be very well attended. I got up early, walked from the hotel to the convention center with plenty of time to spare, and found my way to the appointed room.

When I arrived, I saw it was a tiny room. Maybe twenty chairs were set up. A little screen filled the front of the room, a little projector pointed at it. I asked around to confirm I was in the right place. I was.

The facilitator signed me in, gave me my name tag, and handed me the schedule. I scanned the list of presenters.

Oh. The names. The all-stars.

I was *so* excited. I'd been reading these folks' research; I'd been keeping tabs on new developments in the field. These were cutting-edge scholars and even a few original theorists. I was thrilled to be in the audience.

The topping on this layered cake of research deliciousness was Bob Mankoff, cartoonist and cartoon editor at the New Yorker. I saw his name on the schedule of presenters and my tummy fluttered with butterflies. I felt like a new guitarist hearing Jimmy Page was going to be on stage. I was so excited.

Slowly, folks trickled in, and I watched. Nobody greeted one another. Nobody cracked a joke. There was no laughter.

It was time to begin. There was something odd going on. Twelve people were scheduled to present. There were 14 of us in the room: the presenters, the facilitator, and me. *I* was the audience.

As each person presented, the others in the room worked on their laptops. Without them as an audience, each presenter presented to *me*. I was the only one listening or making eye contact.

Oh, this research was so dry, dull, boring. The research questions being addressed:

"Is humor rooted in moral or benign violation?"

"What are linguistic explanations for humor?"

"What kind of smiles do chimpanzees show when playing; are those facial muscles altered when aggressive or grimacing?"

"Are there effective neurological interventions for involuntary laughter seizures?"

I made eye contact, listened intently, nodded with grave interest.

I didn't laugh once.

Finally, Mr. Mankoff, that breath of fresh New York City air, got up and presented ambiguous cartoons and described a contest where he had readers submit their own captions. He would read a caption and then discuss the humor theory behind it.

Each caption was funnier than the last. I couldn't stop myself from laughing. I was snickering. Snorting. Chortling. Horse laughing. Donkey braying.

Tears sprayed from eyes. Snot ran from my nose. I was laughing so hard tears ran down my leg. (Yes, I may have peed a little).

My laughter was loudly out of place. Everyone else was still fixedly working at their laptops.

As soon as we broke for lunch, Mr. Mankoff made a bee-line for me. "Who're you eating lunch with?" he asked. As I was still stunned by his celebrity status and blankly blinking at him, he took my hand and said, "You're eating with me." We ate our sandwiches outside the convention center in the fresh San Diego sunshine.

Overall, the day was lovely, but not at all what I'd expected.

After I returned home, I reflected on the conference and I realized how dissatisfying it was to see all of that academic posturing and poor sportsmanship in a field as potentially joy-filled as humor. I knew there had to be something better.

I got back to my office that Monday and googled "humor" and "therapy." As a psychotherapist, I saw how valuable laughter and humor were in a therapeutic setting. I just wasn't sure what I'd find in my search.

What I found was the Association of Applied and Therapeutic Humor (AATH.org). I immediately signed up for their conference in chilly Chicago, and while hoping for a better experience than the last time, I still readied myself to be sadly disappointed again.

But instead of being disappointed, I found my *tribe*. This was a group of people who loved laughter and who understood the therapeutic benefits of humor. They were interested in *using* humor; not just studying it.

There were educators, social workers, physicians, psychologists, ministers and priests, therapeutic clowns, recreational, occupational, and psychotherapists, laughter leaders, motivational speakers, and myriad other professions represented. They were supportive of one another, celebrating new research, taking notes on one another's presentations, and cheering everyone on with laughter and good humor.

But there was one topic in that conference that particularly stood out. I wanted to study humor, but my past research had focused on grief and bereavement. Was there a way to combine them? Could adversity and humor coexist?

I attended a breakout session offered by Dr. Chaya Ostrower, who had completed her PhD through Tel Aviv University. Her dissertation was "Humor as a defense mechanism in the Holocaust."

The room was crowded, standing room only. I felt my heart pound with nervous anticipation.

What would she tell us? Could even Holocaust victims use humor in the face of such an atrocity? Would she tell us that humor and suffering could not co-occur? Would she inform us there was no place for humor in that depth of human despair?

Dr. Ostrower gently walked us through her research process. She interviewed fifty-five survivors of the ghettos, concentration camps and/or death camps.

She asked them a simple question: "Can you describe, or tell about, humor in the Holocaust?" She defined humor as: "Anything that made you laugh or smile during the Holocaust." Then she recorded their responses.

The answers were so dark, so brutally honest and painful. Yet some of their stories made me laugh out loud. I felt the need to clamp my hand over my mouth to stop from laughing.

Survivors told of jokes about the cattle cars, being gassed, turned into soap, about being shaved, deloused. They shared a lot of humor about themselves and about their situations. They also joked about other people in the camps, about the guards, and of course, about the Nazis.

Some of the responses were profound. Forgive me for the uninterrupted quotations that follow, but their answers warrant direct reporting and not paraphrasing:

...When I was interviewed for Spielberg and they asked me what I thought was the reason I survived, they probably expected me to answer good fortune or other things. I said that I thought it was laughter and humor, not to take things the way we were living but to dress them up as something different. That was what helped me. I wasn't thinking about miracles and wasn't thinking anything. I only thought how not to take things seriously... and I guess it [this attitude] helped me. Because it was absurd all that time, it was unconceivable, that they could do those things to people.

...Humor was one of the integral ingredients of mental perseverance. This mental perseverance was the condition for a will to live, to put it in a nutshell. This I am telling you as a former prisoner. However little it was, however sporadic, however spontaneous, it was very important, very important. Humor and satire played a tremendous role, in my opinion. It was a cemetery all right and exactly for that reason, the mere fact that we wanted somehow to preserve our personality, [when] they wanted to make robots out of us.

...Look, the ghetto showed that people have great vitality, as soon as a moment's time passed separating one trauma from the other, people were already laughing, they maybe even laughed more.

...This was the integral part of our inner, mental struggle for our human identity, the fact that we could still laugh at things like these.

Look, without humor we would all have committed suicide. We made fun of everything. What I'm actually saying is that that helped us remain human, even under hard conditions.

Dr. Ostrower summarized her research for us as we sat in stunned silence. There was one conclusion in particular that resonated so deeply with me: The use of humor during the Holocaust didn't change the objective atrocity and horror, but the use of humor reduced the subjective experience of it. Humor allowed the prisoners to cope; it provided them an escape.

Viktor Frankl, himself a Holocaust survivor, in *Man's Search for Meaning*, writes, "It is well known that humor, more than anything else in the human make-up, can afford an aloofness and an ability to rise above any situation, even if only for a few seconds." "Humor was another of the soul's weapons in the fight for self-preservation."

As a psychology professor, I can't end this section without talking about Freud again. Yes, he wrote about "Mourning and Melancholia," but he also wrote "Jokes and Their Relationship to the Unconscious."

In this article he writes, "Humor is not resigned; it is rebellious. It signifies the triumph not only of the ego but also of the pleasure-principle, which is strong enough to assert itself here in the face of the adverse real circumstances."

Humor doesn't change the circumstances of our grief. It allows us to cope with it. Humor lends us a reprieve from our sorrow.

How do we grieve with good humor?

When my mother died, my siblings, my dad, and I were absolutely unprepared for it. It was a car crash on my father's birthday. She had painted him a picture that waited, ungiven, in her studio. They had plans for later that day. They had plans for that month. They had plans for retirement; plans for the rest of their lives.

The days leading up to the funeral were somber and hard. My sister and I picked out her burial dress. My brothers selected her casket. We collaborated on the hymns and scriptures for the funeral. We cried some, but mostly we were in shock.

At the funeral, we filled the front couple rows (there are a lot of us). I don't remember much about the service, except the pastor, in the middle of this very serious Presbyterian affair, stopped it all and said, "I'd like you to turn to a neighbor and share a favorite story about Trudy."

My dad, my siblings, and I—we couldn't participate. We were just too sad. So, we just sat there and listened to the din. First there were sniffles and whispers. Then there were giggles and chuckles. Then there were snorts and guffaws. It felt like the walls of the church itself were shaking with laughter.

I was stunned. I couldn't believe it. You mean to tell me I'm allowed to laugh? Laughter was permitted in my grief?

My mother would drive up to visit me at college for a few days, and when we'd go to the grocery store, I'd fill my cart with supplies for the week. At the cash register, I'd unload my cart onto the conveyer belt, and under the cereal boxes there was an enema kit.

Under the toilet paper she'd hidden a pack of women's disposable underwear. Under the bag of apples was a box of condoms.

I'd hand each embarrassing item to the clerk and explain that I'd changed my mind on that item, all while my mother innocently thumbed through a magazine, pretending she had nothing to do with my shame.

Only once was I quick enough to say, "Mother, you got the wrong size of your disposable underpants. We can't get these for you today," as I handed them back to the cashier.

When I was still in high school, there was a day she was running late and needed to cook dinner but hadn't been to the store in a while. She decided to make spaghetti, but there was no hamburger in the fridge for the sauce. Knowing my dad liked meat sauce, she grabbed the hotdogs out of the bottom drawer of the fridge, tossed them in the blender, and hit puree.

This meal was so disgusting, even she refused to eat it. However, my parents were both born during the Great Depression, so food in our house was never discarded. She took all the leftovers (there was a lot), put them in a freezer container, labeled it "wiener spaghetti," and froze it.

After that, if she was running late or just couldn't be bothered to cook, she'd wait until my dad was soon to arrive home from work to pull out the wiener spaghetti, put it on the counter, and leave it there to defrost. He would come in through the back door, see that culinary crime defrosting, and suggest he take her out for dinner.

Both were in on the joke.

When they died and we cleared out the freezer, that thing was a solid block of unrecognizable freezer burn and ice from being so repeatedly thawed and refrozen.

Writing these stories, I already feel closer to her; to him. I feel reconnected and lighter.

Is it okay to grieve with humor? Oh, my friend, it is imperative.

What we know in the field of grief is that most people grieve quite effectively. They experience the emotions of grief, but the impact isn't so severe that it impedes their ability to continue to live their lives.

We've talked about resilience and coping as two factors that help people navigate through their grief. But there is research that shows that good humor also helps us grieve well.

For example, Bonanno (2004) says that using humor in the context of grief can be positive. It can be profoundly beneficial when we are speaking about or remembering a deceased loved one with genuine laughter and smiles.

This kind of humor related to remembrance not only predicts better adjustment, but also more positive responses from others (Bonanno & Keltner, 1997). Such practice can allow for more connection with friends and family members who are walking alongside us.

If you recall the tasks of grief from Chapter Two (Worden, 2008), we want to establish an enduring connection with the deceased by connecting with them again. Using humor is a good way to do this.

When I was chatting with Scott's best friend the other day, we reminisced about Scott's way of telling dad jokes, then smiling and looking around to see who was laughing. I thought his smile was so cute: so proud and full of joy. Remembering this brings him back to me.

If I dwell on times that weren't so sweet, I feel his absence acutely.

I see this in the same way I see my relationship with God. When I focus my attention on how I've sinned against God, how I've hurt Him, I turn away. I feel aggrieved, wounded, distressed. Even remembering my past sins, while I believe they are forgiven, causes me to feel those emotions again—pain, shame, regret—and I again feel separated from God.

When I focus on how Scott and I fought, when I remember how I hurt him, I feel so far from him. I am crushed under waves of pain, shame, regret. My grief intensifies each time I wallow in a place of remembering how I may have failed him.

But in my relationship with God, I am rejoined when I focus on my salvation. If I can center my attention on gratitude, on my joy, my eternal hope, I feel reconnected to Him.

Remember Philippians 4:8 from earlier in this chapter? "Finally, brothers and sisters, whatever is true, whatever is noble, whatever is right, whatever is pure, whatever is lovely, whatever is admirable—if anything is excellent or praiseworthy—*think about such things* and the God of peace will be with you." The things we choose to dwell on will affect our emotions. Gratitude, joy, hope, and all that which is true, noble, right and pure? Let's choose these things, and we will find peace.

Similarly, when I set my focus on how Scott and I laughed together, played together, how we were silly, my heart feels warm and full again. When I focus on his beautiful traits; the ways he was noble and right and admirable, how we loved each other and celebrated each other—to me, this is using good humor in grief. This is my way of reconnecting with him.

I'm not the only one who thinks using humor in grief is a good idea. After researching the topic of communication of humor during bereavement, Booth-Butterfield, Wanzer, Weil and Krezmien (2014) write:

Based on these findings, encouraging and supporting humor and laughter to occur naturally during bereavement interactions is to be recommended. Such coping methods can help ease both the physical and psychological symptoms of grief, and we may best serve the bereaved by affording them safe space and support where they can recall happy memories of their loved one as well as experiencing the full range of emotions that accompany loss (p.14).

In the next and final chapter, we will talk about ways to find meaning and purpose in our suffering. This is the process where our hope is manifested in tangible ways.

Meaning and Transformation

I was enrolled in a class called "Theology of Suffering" during my fall semester of my junior year of college. As part of the assignments for the course, we were to record our thoughts, feelings, and experiences on suffering and submit a journal each week for the professor to review. I used a Mickey Mouse notebook and waxed poetic about God and the meaning of suffering.

My professor, Deena Candler, was also the campus chaplain, and her gentle, humble spirit was the best fit for this really difficult exploration of a really sensitive topic. With great patience, she encouraged me in most areas and challenged me in a few.

The first half of the course, as she assigned us Elie Wiesel's *Night,* Viktor Frankl's *Man's Search for Meaning,* Harold Kushner's *When Bad Things Happen to Good People,* and of course, the book of Job, I read through these books with intellectual curiosity. What does God have to do with suffering? Why do we suffer? Is suffering an absolute evil? When might it be good?

Early on Tuesday morning of midterms that semester, my mother was killed. I watched my strong adult brothers decimated by it. I saw my father sink into a dark chasm of grief. My sister called me nightly in tears. And me? Oh. I was angry.

Suddenly, I had skin in this game. It was no longer an academic pursuit to wonder about who God was in the midst of suffering. I needed to know. I demanded answers.

I took that stupid Mickey Mouse notebook, wrote out my rage and fury about that week of my mother's death and funeral, and stapled the pages together so Professor Candler couldn't view them. I threw it on her desk and glared at her.

She nodded.

This was personal. God had some answering to do. Trite answers were *not* going to cut it.

Is pain bad? Is suffering evil?

I have no answers. Even now. But I have stories. I've read some smart writers. Here's where I am right now with this question about the meaning of suffering and pain.

Let's Talk about Pain for a Quick Minute

I'm just going to say it like it is, and I'm sorry if I offend. We are a bunch of big babies. We are pansies. We are terrified of pain. We are told by advertisers to take medicine at the first sign of pain. Doctors prescribe morphine-based drugs for simple medical conditions.

Remember from the chapter on humor, I told the story of Norman Cousins? His medical condition, which he treated with laughter and positive emotion, was excruciatingly painful. It was unbearable at times, but he chose to endure it and not anesthetize it because he viewed the pain as important information. He believed his pain served a purpose.

In his book, he despaired at how quickly we as Americans try to numb it. We flee from it. We medicate it too quickly without ever trying to understand where it comes from. He writes,

> *We know very little about pain and what we don't know makes it hurt all the more. Indeed, no form of illiteracy in the United States is so widespread or costly as ignorance about pain—what it is, what causes it, how to deal with it without panic. Almost everyone can rattle off the names of at least a dozen drugs that can deaden pain from every conceivable cause—all the way from headaches to hemorrhoids.*

Have you ever thought that pain can be a blessing? Pain serves a purpose. It is our body's signal system that something is wrong. If we burn our hand on the stove, the body signals the brain, telling us there's an injury that needs attention.

Pain can be a way of congratulating us for hard work. The ache of my arms, back, and legs after a good, hard day of raking leaves feels gratifying. We intensify our pain on purpose when we do heavy leg lifts or repetitive arm pulls at the gym. Afterwards we feel accomplished, knowing that pain will lead to greater fitness.

Pain can caution us of danger. A burning fire in a fireplace is comforting from a safe and cozy distance, but if we get too close, pain will send out a warning to move away so we don't get hurt.

Sometimes, we even increase our pain for relief. When a tooth is coming in, a baby will bite down on the area of pain and create counter-pressure to cause a different kind of pain.

A mild pain tells us there is a minor issue; major pain tells us something significant is happening. A scratch on your skin from playing with your kitten will be less significant an event than a broken leg.

There is a disorder called Congenital Insensitivity to Pain with Anhidrosis, or CIPA, where the child is born with an inability to feel pain or extreme temperatures. Parents have to watch the child with CIPA so she doesn't bite her own hands too deeply to cause serious injury. Parents have to make sure the child doesn't play so rough he breaks a bone without knowing it; or that she doesn't dip her hand in the boiling water just to see what the bubbles feel like.

What this disorder tells us is that pain not only warns us of what's gone wrong in the body, but pain also cautions us not to take unnecessary risks.

In this respect, pain is a gift. If we didn't know we were hurt, we wouldn't attend to the injury. Without pain, we wouldn't protect ourselves.

During the course of our marriage, Scott had a kidney stone; I gave birth to two children and miscarried four. Scott's doctors told him the pain of a kidney stone is close to, or perhaps even the equivalent to the pain of childbirth. He was happy to remind me of this when I was experiencing the pain of labor. (Husbands, don't ever do this; it's very ill-advised.)

After the fact, though, I sympathized with him. Kidney stones and childbirth are both excruciatingly painful. But there is one primary difference between the two: the pain of a kidney stone feels pointless, while the pain of having a baby carries profound meaning and significance.

Scott was clear he never wanted to have another kidney stone and wished he'd not had that one. I, on the other hand, would go through labor 100 times over for either one of my kids.

The pain of childbirth was negligible and forgettable compared to the profound presence of my children in my life. Even the pain of miscarriage, both the emotional and physical hurt, felt like a beautiful, sacred pain.

We can endure any kind of pain if we know it carries meaning; a purpose.

And yet, C. S. Lewis writes,

When I think of pain—of anxiety that gnaws like fire and loneliness that spreads out like a desert... of dull aches that blacken our whole landscape or sudden nauseating pains that knock a man's heart out at one blow, of pains that seem already intolerable and then are suddenly increased.... If I knew any way of escape, I would crawl through sewers to find it (p. 65).

Grief is hard and, at times, ugly. When we are in the depths of despair, howling out to God in our pain, we are reduced to such a dark place. We don't want to bear it.

Who am I when I am in my darkest place, when I am curled up in a fetal position, hiding under the covers and staining my pillow with tears?

Who am I when I'm not writing a book about humor and resilience and coping?

I am a whimpering, sniveling cry-baby.

Instead of tolerating my grief, I want to be happy again. I struggle and rage against the idea that I can't be happy all the time. Why doesn't God seem all that interested in my happiness?

Lewis writes,

We want, in fact, not so much a Father in Heaven as a grandfather in heaven—a senile benevolence who, as they say, "liked to see young people enjoying themselves" and whose plan for the universe was simply that it might be truly said at the end of each day, "a good time was had by all." (p. 21)

God isn't invested in something so shallow and fleeting as our happiness. He's solely invested in our relationship with Him. Sometimes pain is the path that leads us to Him.

Along the road that sometimes involves pain, He promises joy.

Not happiness.

Joy.

Pain can be a transformative gift. God doesn't lead us away from pain. He allows us to encounter it. He walks along with us through it. But that means we must still endure it.

As my beloved friend, Dr. Boyd Seevers gently reminded me the other day: "God rarely wastes pain."

Two months after Scott died, my children and I visited a relative in prison for Thanksgiving. As we sat waiting for them to be called out from their cell, we watched offenders come into the visitors' area; they smiled and laughed and shook hands with their friends and family members. Wonderful reunions all around us. Happy Thanksgiving! Holiday Cheer!

Then it hit me: Each one of these individuals had committed a felony. Some of them were murderers. Others were found guilty of sexual assault. There were embezzlers. Thieves. Drug dealers.

My sweet husband volunteered every spare minute he had to work with kids and horses. Most of the expendable income we had he'd spend on rescuing horses from abuse and neglect. A few evenings a week, he would work with children with disabilities to help them ride horses. He'd teach horseback riding lessons to kids at risk. He'd sweat through hot summer days to teach kids to ride at Make-a-Wish camps.

But these felons were all alive. My altruistic husband was dead.

These felons were kissing their spouses. I would never feel his lips on mine again.

These felons were hugging their kids. Laughing with them. Playing board games. They might be out in time to see their children get married and become parents themselves.

My daughter would walk down the aisle alone. My son would become a fatherless father.

In that moment, I realized the world was *not* fair.

There was no justice. Not for me. Not for my children.

I can't describe to you how earth-shattering this was to me.

Making Sense of This

The way we experience suffering is directly related to our beliefs about it. Our worldviews impact our grief. We hold certain assumptions about the world, ourselves, and others. We believe the world works a certain way, and that belief system helps us feel safe and in control.

I wanted a just world. I wanted the world to be fair—where good people lived and bad people died. That seemed simple enough. But nothing about my life felt fair or just.

In this section, I am going to write through the lens of my personal faith. Frankly, I can't make sense of death or life or human existence without looking at them through my faith. I cannot look at suffering without keeping my eyes on my God.

As you read, I encourage you to consider how you understand this content through the lens of your faith, as well.

Do I get what I deserve?

The first Christmas without Scott was hard for me and the kids. To be honest, it was mostly a blur. Honestly, I don't even remember hosting my extended family on Christmas day, but my sister and brother and their families assure me it happened.

The day after Christmas, the kids were both hit with a virulent stomach bug, the dog had diarrhea, and the cat had eaten the rubber tip of a nerf dart that had lodged in his small intestine, requiring emergency surgery. The day after *that*, while driving my daughter home from an appointment during a snow storm, our car spiraled out of control and we ended up in the ditch.

Sitting in our car with the wipers barely keeping the windshield clear of snow, in the deep snow of the ditch, facing oncoming traffic, I immediately thought, "Okay. We're safe. I just need to call Scott to come and get us." Then I remembered he was dead.

After a good long time crying with my daughter, I called a tow truck. It would be hours before they could get to me, so the tow truck driver told me to leave the keys in the car and he'd fetch it when he could.

Then I called my friend. She was so sweet; eager to help. She actually thanked me for asking her. When she pulled up next to us and we climbed in to her warm car, she asked me, "Melissa, what have you done to deserve all of this?"

I know she was kidding, but it felt shamefully familiar. I wondered how many other people were secretly wondering the same thing.

There are many people who believe that we get what we deserve. They believe AIDS victims die because of unsafe practices. They believe people are raped because they dress provocatively (please note that research has shown the number one cause for rape, however, is rapists). They believe that people who suffer have somehow earned that suffering.

Does God give us what we deserve?

Well, no. I can't imagine what in the world I could have done to deserve these great kids of mine. I didn't deserve a husband who loved me as deeply as Scott did. I did nothing to deserve my salvation. I don't deserve to have been born into a variety of privileges. I didn't deserve my loving parents any more than a child of abuse deserves his abusive parents. Do we really get what we deserve?

Did Scott get what was coming to him when his cancer killed him? Did I get what was coming to me by being left behind?

People who hold to this you-get-what-you-deserve belief tend to see God as punitive, score-keeping, and cruel.

This argument falls apart when we see the suffering of small, innocent children. They've done nothing; they warrant no pain. Pediatric oncology wards exist. Children have seizures. Babies are hurt by caregivers.

How can any of this be deserved? What kind of God would deliver this kind of quid pro quo justice that seems so unjust?

Am I being punished?

Maybe God is using pain and suffering to punish us. Is our pain the result of punishment? Is God using it as discipline?

In parenting, we know that punishment is effective when the child knows specifically which rule he broke, how he broke it, and what the consequence is.

An example of this would be: "The rule in this house is 'no hitting.' You hit your brother. The consequence is a time out. You are six years old so you will sit in time out for six minutes, and I will set the timer and I will tell you when you may get up."

Yes, this is adaptive punishment for a clearly stated rule that was broken. Punishing a child for something but *not* telling him what he did wrong is just bad parenting.

So, what am I being punished for as I grieve the death of my beloved? What specifically did I do wrong?

The cancer was an agonizingly painful kind of cancer and death. What exactly did Scott do? I know we are both sinners. But what is the connection between one particular sin and a particular punishment?

What is Multiple Sclerosis punishment for? How about dementia? Is Sudden Infant Death a punishment for something? What was the rule that was broken that would warrant the deadly crash of a family of seven as they were on their way to serve on the mission field?

A reasonable parent would never punish a child but withhold the explanation. Why do we suggest this is a reasonable action of God the Father?

No, this is not the character of God as I understand Him.

What must I learn?

Sometimes I'm told that God inflicts pain, or causes us to suffer, in order to teach us something. What can I learn from this period of grief? This is a great question, but I can't answer it. I don't know. I haven't found the textbook that lays out those lessons.

What are you supposed to learn from the death of your sister? Where's the handbook for that? Is there a manual somewhere that tells us the lessons we must learn from our child's death? I haven't found it. Yet we tell a grieving mother she is to learn something from this but not tell her what the lesson is?

This is not the character of God as I understand Him.

Does God give you more than you can handle?

I've been told that God never gives us more than we can handle. It's burned into decorative wooden wall hangings. It's all over Pinterest with lovely backgrounds: "God doesn't give you more than you can handle."

No? Except for bland memes and tacky wall hangings, where is that *actually* written? Is it in the Bible? Is it in the book of Lamentations, a book so heavy with grief, it's difficult to read? Is it in the Psalms when David is crying out to God in despair?

How about when Jesus is crying out, "My God, My God, why have You forsaken me?"

I don't recall reading in any of the four gospels that someone reached up to pat Jesus on his bloody foot nailed to the cross to whisper, "There, there, Jesus. God never gives you more than you can handle."

In 1 Corinthians 10:13, the Apostle Paul writes, "No temptation has overtaken you that is not common to man. God is faithful, and He will not let you be tempted beyond your ability, but with the temptation He will also provide the way of escape, that you may be able to endure it."

In some translations, temptation is replaced with the word, "test." This is where we learn we will not be tested beyond our ability.

This is the verse that so many people quote to tell you that you won't be given more than you can handle. But Paul isn't even talking about suffering. He is talking about sin. The *test* is about temptation to sin.

No, in fact, Paul tells us we might suffer beyond our limits. In 2 Corinthians 1:8, he writes, "For we do not want you to be ignorant, brothers, of the affliction we experienced in Asia. For we were so utterly burdened *beyond our strength* that we despaired of life itself."

We don't see blame here, though. Nowhere does Paul write, "...and God did this to us because he is a cruel and arbitrary deity." No. We sometimes add that in ourselves.

Tom and Sharon's six-year-old daughter died from E-coli poisoning a few years ago. As they stood next to her little casket, her tiny body in a frilly, white dress with little, red cherries dotting it, arms folded over a favorite doll, Sharon kept looking over at her child, longing to climb into the casket with her and hold her baby one last time.

I stood nearby, cringing as I heard well-meaning mourners handing her parents big, steaming piles of bad theology. As they'd hug Tom and Sharon, they'd say, "God just needed another angel."

They'd inflict deeper wounds by saying, "She's in a better place." To me, the most horrific assurance: "This must have been God's will."

I know the visitors hoped their words would give comfort. They were trying to make sense of this devastating and senseless death. They were desperate to help.

But they were inflicting pain.

They were maligning God.

Who is God in All of This?

What kind of God do you believe in? The kind who gives us what we deserve, but doesn't show us the spreadsheet of our good and bad deeds? The kind of God who punishes us but doesn't tell us what for? The one who is teaching us a painful lesson but gives no information about what we are to learn?

Do you believe in a God who forces us to the brink of our human endurance just to see how much suffering we can take? Do you believe in the God who willfully plucks a beautiful child from the arms of her mother simply because He wants that little girl to himself?

I'm sorry. That's not the God I believe in.

My daughter was struggling after Scott died. She'd have to graduate from high school without him there. College, too. During her senior year, she got a modeling job which allowed her to briefly live in Paris, but her dad wasn't there to be proud of her, to brag about her to anyone within earshot as he was known to do.

She will marry and have children someday, and her dad won't be there to meet and love her family. Her father will be absent in every important event of her life. She will never get to see him again.

One night, through her tears, she asked, "What kind of God thought this was a good idea?"

As her mother, this question devastated me. I had to ask myself, "How can I reintroduce her to the God I believe in? The One Who thinks death is a very *bad* idea."

Here is what I believe. I am not insisting that you believe it, too, but I do invite you to consider it.

I believe the fall of humanity (sin) set in motion a cascade of catastrophic events that result in disease and death today. *This* is the cause of suffering. I believe Jesus was the son of God, I believe that Jesus came to earth as a man, that He died on a cross to pay the price (death) for my sin, and that He rose from the dead. I believe Jesus is my salvation and my source for eternal life.

There are both Roman and Jewish historical documents, in addition to the Bible, that also document the life, ministry, and death of Jesus as well as His resurrection.

During Jesus' ministry on earth, I believe He performed miracles. Many of those miracles involved healing the sick, giving sight to the blind, making the lame walk, and raising people from the dead.

If sickness and death were part of the kingdom of God, would Jesus have fought so hard against it? Would He have bothered to conquer death as His finale?

Based on the ministry of Jesus and how he dedicate his time and energy on earth, I can only conclude that sickness and death are not part of the kingdom of God.

Where is God in the midst of my personal suffering, then?

When the semi that killed my mother crossed four lanes of traffic and rammed her vehicle into the ditch, I believe the heart of God broke first.

When Lazarus died, Jesus wept (John 11:35).

When the first cancer cell divided in my husband's chest, God grieved.

My belief about God is that He is with us. He gives us His comfort. He provides us space and love in which to heal. He walks beside us, and at times, He carries us. He shelters us. He leads us beside the still waters. He lays us down in green pastures. He restores our soul.

God designed us to love Him. He wants to be with us. He seeks us out for relationship. He lavishes His love on us and seeks our love in return.

To quote Archibald MacLeish,

> *Man depends on God for all things; God depends on man for one. Without man's love, God does not exist as God, only as creator, and love is the one thing no one, not even God Himself, can command. It is a free gift, or it is nothing. And it is most itself, most free, when it is offered in spite of suffering, of injustice, and of death.*

God created us solely for relationship with Him, to love Him. Our love is only valuable to Him if we freely choose to love Him – even despite our suffering and pain.

Maybe you believe the world is a fair place and everything works out in the end. Like I used to, maybe you believe that good things happen to good people and bad things happen to bad people. These views of the world help you manage your expectations and see the world as just.

But then your loved one dies and your belief system is shaken to its core.

Can We Answer "Why"?

There are moments in the middle of the dark night when I lie awake and 1 want to know "why." Why did this happen to me? Why did he have to die? Why am I suffering? Why can't I have him with me? Why must I endure this?"

To be fully honest with you (and myself), if the Good Lord stood in front of me and took my face in His hands and explained in perfect Minnesotan English why Scott died, it would not help my grief. Not at all. The perfect and complete answer to my demands of "WHY?" wouldn't suffice, because it still wouldn't take away my pain.

So, I require faith. Faith that someday we will see the purpose of our pain in this transformational process of grief. Richard Rohr says in one of his lectures, "When you are brought to a door of transformation, and you reach out and turn the doorknob, the path behind you straightens. That's what faith does."

Perhaps, rather than demanding to know why we are enduring this pain, a better question to ask is, "Now that he's gone, what can I do about it?"

Perhaps we can ask, "What can I do to create a beautiful result?" "How might I redeem this loss?"

Meaning in our Suffering

Theologians and philosophers often write about finding meaning in our suffering, and I want to set our focus on this now. If pain has purpose, then does suffering also have purpose?

C. S. Lewis writes:

I answer that suffering is not good in itself. What is good in any painful experience is, for the sufferer, his submission to the will of God, and, for the spectators, the compassion aroused and the acts of mercy to which it leads (Lewis, p.69).

When Scott was diagnosed, and he realized it was terminal, he changed. His disposition changed. His priorities shifted. All the parts of him that were concerned with mundane details disappeared.

All that mattered to him was the divine status of those he encountered during his last months. As he was dying, he only concerned himself with how he could help others live life eternally.

He called everyone out on their spiritual lives: "How are you doing right now, Nate? Are you right with God?" Doctors and nurses were invited to talk about their religious faith. Even the guy coming in to empty the sharps container was asked to talk about his spiritual health.

Scott was suffering so much physical pain. The cancer continued eating into his bones and gnawing at his brain and spinal cord. He was saying goodbye to me. He was left wondering who his children would grow up to be and reconciling himself to the fact that he would never know.

But despite that suffering, he wasn't going to mess around. He had a mission. He had a purpose in dying, and he would not waver from it.

Dr. Viktor Frankl was a psychiatrist who was imprisoned at Auschwitz during the Holocaust. He watched his fellow prisoners and saw that, no matter the conditions, no matter the torture or special treatment men received during their time in the camps, some survived while others perished.

Frankl realized that men were able to tolerate their suffering if they were able to attach meaning to it.

After being liberated from the concentration camp, Frankl wrote the book *Man's Search for Meaning*. In it he chronicles what he and his fellow prisoners endured:

Dostoevski said once, 'There is only one thing I dread: not to be worthy of my sufferings.' These words frequently came to my mind after I became acquainted with those martyrs whose behavior in camp, whose suffering and death, bore witness to the fact that the last inner freedom cannot be lost. It can be said that they were worthy of their sufferings; the way they bore their suffering was a genuine inner achievement. It is this spiritual freedom— which cannot be taken away—that makes life meaningful and purposeful."

In the face of a most devastating existence, these men lived and died well by finding meaning in their suffering.

Nietzsche writes, "He who has a *why* to live for can bear with almost any *how.*"

When the Americans came and freed the camps, Frankl describes his liberation. As he walked down a country road with flowering meadows and singing larks, he was stunned by beauty and freedom.

He dropped to his knees and had only one sentence to proclaim, "I called to the Lord from my narrow prison, and He answered me in the freedom of space."

I think about what Scott suffered in those 144 days, from the day they found the first tumor to the day he died. As hard as it was, Scott knew his reason for living and he embraced his purpose in death. He was able to endure the "how" of his death because he believed in the "why." He resolutely believed that "...all things work together for good to them that love God, to them who are the called according to his purpose" (Romans 8:28).

Scott called to his Lord in the narrow prison of disease and was answered in the freedom of Heaven.

As Viktor Frankl reflected on his experiences in the concentration camps, what he witnessed, what he endured, his final reflection was this: "The crowning experience of all, for the homecoming man, is the wonderful feeling that, after all he has suffered, there is nothing he need fear any more—except his God."

If there is only one thing to dread, to not be worthy of your suffering, then perhaps it is time to reflect: What is the purpose in your pain? What are you called to do, or be, through your suffering? What is the meaning in your loss? How can you be transformed through this pain?

Shortly after Scott died, my son and I were in the car, and he looked up at me with big, teary brown eyes and asked, "Mom, if you had one wish, wouldn't you just want to take away our suffering?"

I paused. I prayed. I breathed.

I surprised him with my answer: "No, baby, I don't think I would."

I'm not a monster. I would never choose to watch my children suffer. Yet I wouldn't take away their pain because their grief is beautiful and profound. It is a mark of how dear and beautiful their father was to them.

I can't bring him back. I wouldn't want to. I believe he is in Heaven, and how selfish of me to want him to leave that, to come back here (have you ever visited Minnesota in January? You don't wish that on your worst enemies).

Yes, my children watched their father get sick. They watched him fight really hard. They watched him suffer. They watched him die.

And I have watched my children. They have emerged into stronger, fuller, more vibrant versions of themselves because of this grief. They have reached out to their friends. They have articulated their emotions. They have loved each other deeply. They have supported me emotionally.

When I cry, my teens come and sit with me until I can smile again. They send me funny memes to cheer me. Tease me and laugh together to lift me up.

They have figured out how to navigate conflict with a healthy perspective around the issues that really matter in life.

When my boy asked if I would take away this pain, I couldn't say yes. This life isn't supposed to be free from adversity.

This life is a pilgrimage. Phil Cosineau calls this life "a transformative journey to a sacred center," full of hardships, darkness, and peril.

Parker Palmer says, "In the tradition of pilgrimage, those hardships are seen not as accidental but as integral to the journey itself."

Now, I'm not much of a gardener. Mostly my plants suffer from dire neglect. They would fare much better if they could whine and complain for food as loudly as my kids do. But I did take a horticulture class in high school, so that must count for something in this next analogy.

If I plant a seedling in the ground, and I religiously water it, protect it from strong winds, monitor the sunlight so the plant doesn't scorch, and I provide all its nutrients right at the surface of the soil, I will have a healthy plant.

But the root system has no need to tunnel deep. There's no adversity, no challenge, no suffering. The plant will appear healthy but it won't produce much. It won't demonstrate hardiness. The fruit will be small, and any taxing stress on the stems may harm it.

So, what happens when real adversity occurs? What happens when there is a drought? A strong wind? The force of a storm will lift the plant with the shallow roots up out of the ground and toss it away because there's nothing to tether that plant down.

On the other hand, if you garden like I do (with inattention and casual neglect), that seedling will have to burrow its roots down deep into the ground to find water, nutrients, to get the sustenance it needs to thrive. Scorching sunshine, too much shade: these things will force this plant to endure. The result is a hardy plant. The fruit is large, the stems thick. The roots are deep.

What happens to the plant when serious adversity hits? In the storm, that plant isn't going anywhere. In a drought, it knows where to get its water.

My children's grief is doing the same thing for them. They are facing adversity in their grief: mourning the death of their dad, watching the other sibling suffer, watching their mother cry.

This is making them dig deeper to understand the world. They are struggling to understand the character of God. In this process, they are becoming two strong, hardy, resilient kids.

My son, like me, like you, like all of us, wanted the pain to be taken away and wanted to be happy again. But nowhere are we promised happiness. It is found nowhere in scripture.

Paul Tripp writes, "We forget that God's primary goal is not changing our situations so we can be happy, but changing us through our situations so that we will be holy."

You see, even as we have navigated through our grief, the world hasn't changed. Circumstances haven't changed. We have changed.

Our pain is sacred.

Through it, we are transformed.

That, my beloved reader, is the goal of grief work.

Appendix I: Additional Grief Resources

General Grief

- Griefnet.org – (support for adults grieving a loss) **http://www.griefnet.org/**
- GriefShare (seminars, support groups, and daily encouragements) **https://www.griefshare.org/**
- Grieving.com (chat rooms for various forms of loss) **https://forums.grieving.com/**
- Open to Hope (articles, podcasts, online support) **https://www.opentohope.com**
- What's Your Grief? (Resources, information, e-courses) **https://whatsyourgrief.com/**

Suicide, Homicide, Traumatic Loss

- American Association of Suicidality **https://www.suicidology.org/**
- American Foundation for Suicide Prevention - Support for suicide survivors **https://afsp.org/**
- The National Center for Victims of Crime **http://victimsofcrime.org/**
- Tragedy Assistance Program for Survivors (TAPS) **https://www.taps.org/**

Death of a child

- American Childhood Cancer Organization **https://www.acco.org/**
- The Compassionate Friends – (support after the death of a child) **https://www.compassionatefriends.org/**
- First Candle SIDS Alliance (online support groups for families) **https://firstcandle.org/**
- National Center for Missing and Exploited Children **http://www.missingkids.com/**
- National Organization of Parents of Murdered Children, INC **http://www.pomc.com/**
- Unspoken Grief (resources for reproductive losses) **http://unspokengrief.com/**

Death of a Spouse

- Cancer Care (spousal bereavement support) **https://www.cancercare.org/support_groups/57-spouse_partner_s_bereavement_support_group**

- **National Widower's Organization** (Support for men grieving a loss) **https://nationalwidowers.org/**

- Parents Without Partners (an organization for single parents and their children) **https://www.parentswithoutpartners.org/**

Support for Children

- Hellogrief.org (support for adults and kids grieving a loss) **http://www.hellogrief.org/**

- The National Alliance for Grieving Children **https://childrengrieve.org/**

- Scholastic Children and Grief Support Resources **http://www.scholastic.com/childrenandgrief/**

Mental Health Resources

- Addiction Resource Drug Abuse Hotline **https://addictionresource.com/addiction-and-rehab-hotlines/**

- American Foundation for Suicide Prevention **https://afsp.org/**

- Black Mental Health Alliance **http://blackmentalhealth.com/**

- Focus on the Family's Christian Counselors Network (find a Christian Counselor near you) **https://ccn.thedirectorywidget.com/**

- Make It Ok **https://makeitok.org/**

- National Domestic Violence Hotline **https://www.thehotline.org/**

- National Resource Center for Hispanic Mental Health **http://www.nrchmh.org/**

- Psychology Today "Find a Therapist" **https://www.psychologytoday.com/us**

- Rural Mental Health Information Hub **https://www.ruralhealthinfo.org/topics/mental-health**

- Substance Abuse and Mental Health Services Administration (SAMHSA) treatment facilities locator and Suicide Help **https://www.findtreatment.samhsa.gov/**

- Suicide Prevention Lifeline 1-800-273-TALK (8255)

References

Am I Normal?

Clark, A. E., & Georgellis, Y. (2013). Back to baseline in Britain: Adaptation in the British household panel survey. *Economica, 80*(319), 496-512. doi:10.1111/ecca.12007

Holmes, T. H., & Rahe, R. H. (1967). The social readjustment rating scale. *Journal of Psychosomatic Research, 11*(2), 213-218. doi:10.1016/0022-3999(67)90010-4

Tasks of Grief

Bowlby, J. (1961). Processes of mourning. *International Journal of Psycho-Analysis, 42,* 317-340.

Freud, S. (1924). Mourning and melancholia. *The Psychoanalytic Review (1913-1957), 11,* 77.

Klass, D., Silverman, P. R., & Nickman, S. L. (1996). Continuing bonds: New understandings of grief. New York: Routledge.

Kübler-Ross, E. (1973; 1969). On death and dying. London;New York;: Routledge.

Lindemann, E. (1944). Symptomatology and management of acute grief. *American Journal of Psychiatry, 101*(2), 141-148. doi:10.1176/ajp.101.2.141

Parkes, C. M. (1970). The first year of bereavement: A longitudinal study of the reaction of London widows to the death of their husbands. *Psychiatry, 33*(4), 444-467.

Rando,T. (1991). How to go on living when someone you love dies. New York: Bantam Books.

Worden, J. W. (2008). Grief counseling and grief therapy, fourth edition: A handbook for the mental health practitioner (4th ed.). New York: Springer Publishing Company.

Resilience

Bonanno, G. A., Wortman, C. B., & Nesse, R. M. (2004). Prospective patterns of resilience and maladjustment during widowhood. *Psychology and Aging, 19*(2), 260-271. doi:10.1037/0882-7974.19.2.260

Brunwasser, S. M., Freres, D. R., & Gillham, J. E. (2018). Youth cognitive-behavioral depression prevention: Testing theory in a randomized controlled trial. *Cognitive Therapy and Research, 42*(4), 468-482. doi:10.1007/s10608-018-9897-6

Martínez-Martí, M. L., & Ruch, W. (2017). Character strengths predict resilience over and above positive affect, self-efficacy, optimism, social support, self-esteem, and life satisfaction. *The Journal of Positive Psychology, 12*(2), 110-119. doi:10.1080/17439760.2016.1163403

Peterson, C., Seligman, M. E. P., & NetLibrary, I. (2004). Character strengths and virtues: A handbook and classification. New York;Washington, DC;: American Psychological Association.

Samson, A. C., Glassco, A. L., Lee, I. A., & Gross, J. J. (2014). Humorous coping and serious reappraisal: Short-term and longer-term effects. *Europe's Journal of Psychology, 10*(3), 571-581. doi:10.5964/ejop.v10i3.730

Sandberg, S., & Grant, A. M. (2017). Option B: Facing adversity, building resilience, and finding joy (First ed.). New York: Alfred A. Knopf.

Schachter, S., & Singer, J. (1962). Cognitive, social, and physiological determinants of emotional state. *Psychological Review, 69*(5), 379-399. doi:10.1037/h0046234

Coping and Creating Change

Cameron, J. (2016). The artist's way. Penguin.

Ellis, A., & MacLaren, C. (1998). Rational emotive behavior therapy: A therapist's guide. Impact Publishers.

Frankl, V. E. (1985). Man's search for meaning. Simon and Schuster.

Lamott, A. (2000). Traveling mercies: Some thoughts on faith. Anchor.

Humor

Berk, L. S., Felten, D. L., Tan, S. A., Bittman, B. B., & Westengard, J. (2001). Modulation of neuroimmune parameters during the eustress of humor-associated mirthful laughter. *Alternative Therapies in Health and Medicine, 7*(2), 62.

Berk, R. A. (2002). Humor as an instructional defibrillator: Evidence-based techniques in teaching and assessment (First ed.). Sterling, Va: Stylus.

Bonanno, G. (2004). Loss, trauma, & human resilience. *American Psychologist, 59*, 20–28.

Bonanno, G., & Keltner, D. (1997). Facial expressions of emotion and the course of conjugal bereavement. *Journal of Abnormal Psychology, 106*, 126–137.

Booth-Butterfield, M., Bekelja Wanzer, M., Weil, N., & Krezmien, E. (2014) Communication of humor during bereavement: Intrapersonal and interpersonal emotion management strategies, *Communication Quarterly, 62*:4,436-454, DOI: 10.1080/01463373.2014.922487

Cousins, Norman. Anatomy of an Illness as Perceived by the Patient : Reflections on Healing and Regeneration . New York: Norton, 1979. Print.

Driver, J. L., & Gottman, J. M. (2004). Daily marital interactions and positive affect during marital conflict among newlywed couples. *Family Process, 43*(3), 301-314. doi:10.1111/j.1545-5300.2004.00024.x

Freud, S. (1905) Jokes and Their Relationship to the Unconscious. Deuticke

Gray, A. W., Parkinson, B., & Dunbar, R. I. (2015). Laughter's influence on the intimacy of self-disclosure. *Human Nature : An Interdisciplinary Biosocial Perspective, 26*(1), 28-43. DOI: 10.1007/s12110-015-9225-8

Maemura, Y., & Horita, M. (2012). Humour in negotiations: A pragmatic analysis of humour in simulated negotiations. *Group Decision and Negotiation, 21*(6), 821-838. doi:10.1007/s10726-011-9251-9

McGettigan, C et al. (2015) "Individual differences in laughter perception reveal roles for mentalizing and sensorimotor systems in the evaluation of emotional authenticity." *Cerebral Cortex. 25*(1), 246–257.

Mesmer-Magnus, J., Glew, D. J., & Visweswaran, C. (2012). A meta-analysis of positive humor in the workplace. *Journal of Managerial Psychology, 27*(2), 155-190. doi:10.1108/02683941211199554

Miller, M., & Fry, W. F. (2009). The effect of mirthful laughter on the human cardiovascular system. *Medical Hypotheses, 73*(5), 636-639. doi:10.1016/j.mehy.2009.02.044

Mobbs, D., Greicius, M. D., Abdel-Azim, E., Menon, V., & Reiss, A. L. (2003). Humor modulates the mesolimbic reward centers. *Neuron, 40*(5), 1041-1048. doi:10.1016/S0896-6273(03)00751-7

Ostrower, C., (2015). Humor as a defense mechanism during the Holocaust. *Interpretation: a Journal of Bible and Theology, 69*(2), 183-195. 10.1177/0020964314564830

Provine, R. R. (2004). Laughing, tickling, and the evolution of speech and self. *Current Directions in Psychological Science, 13*(6), 215-218. doi:10.1111/j.0963-7214.2004.00311.x

Selye, H. (1956). The stress of life. New York, NY, US: McGraw-Hill.

Meaning and Purpose

Cousins, N. (1979) Anatomy of an Illness as Perceived by the Patient: Reflections on Healing and Regeneration. New York: Norton, Print.

Cossneau, P.(2012) The Art of Pilgrimage: The Seeker's Guide to Making Travel Sacred. San Fransisco: Canari Press.

Frankl, V. E. (1985). Man's search for meaning. Simon and Schuster.

Kushner, H. S. (2007). When bad things happen to good people. Anchor.

Lewis, C.S. (1961) A Grief Observed. New York: Harper Collins.

Lewis, C. S. (2001) The Problem of Pain. San Francisco: Harper Collins.

Palmer, Parker J. Let Your Life Speak : Listening for the Voice of Vocation. San Francisco: Jossey-Bass, 2001.

Rohr, R. & Feister, J. (2001) Hope against darkness: The Transforming vision of Saint Francis in an age of anxiety. *Franciscan Media, 69*, 81-82

Tripp, P. D. (2002). Instruments in the Redeemer's hands. *Religion, 9*(781935), 273066.

Wiesel, E. (2006). Night (Vol. 55). Macmillan.

Acknowledgments

Thank you, Tanya Grosz, for getting me started and believing in me. Thanks, Leah Nelson for the content help. Thank you, Emily Jacobs, for the encouragement. Thanks, Erica Sundvall, for removing some of my excess exclamation points!!! You are diligent and smart. Thank you, Traci Mielke DePree, for your insight and skill. You are firm but kind, and I am grateful.

To my friends, Mike and Linda Fournier, thank you for the unwavering support of me and for your deep love for the Morklets. Thank you, Sue Payne, for supporting me through the first year of deepest grief. You sustained me and I am deeply grateful to you.

Thanks to Barry Jensen for fixing my snowblower and mowing my lawn, hence clearing the way for me to write. Thanks to Libby Jensen for being the one to think, "Alpaca brandy for Melissa!" Jackie Hempeck, thank you for the weighted blanket love for my children, and thanks, Gary Hempeck, for always being happy to see me. To Carl and Pamela Billings, thank you for giving me the bicycle that has become my therapy. Thank you, Doug Anderson. You were a constant source of laughter. Thank you, Harald Eide Ellingsen, for the music that allowed me to write.

My love and gratitude also goes to my siblings. Brenda, Mike, Ran, Jeff, Brad, Dave and Greg. Thanks for holding me to a standard that is impossible to meet, and then teasing me mercilessly for falling short. Also, thanks for the cheers and support. You are my greatest, fiercest, most loyal allies.

Caroline Mellor Baartman, you were my source of great strength through the worst of it. I am forever grateful for you. I will never be able to repay you.

To my children, thanks for the permission to tell our story. You are the two bravest people I know.

Finally, to my mother, Trudy; my dad, Marion; to my unborn children; to my friends who have gone before me; and to my beloved husband, Scott: may your deaths not be in vain.

Love,
Melissa

The Sovereign Lord has given me an instructed tongue
to know the words to sustain the weary.
He wakens me, morning by morning.
He wakens my ear as one being taught.
Isaiah 50:4

CPSIA information can be obtained
at www.ICGtesting.com
Printed in the USA
LVHW041518101019
633803LV00002B/375/P